TEST ITEM FILE

Lisa Miles Bunkowski

THE WORLD'S HISTORY

THIRD EDITION

Howard Spodek

Temple University

PEARSON

Prentice
Hall

Upper Saddle River, New Jersey 07458

© 2006 by PEARSON EDUCATION, INC.
Upper Saddle River, New Jersey 07458

10 9 8 7 6 5 4 3 2 1

ISBN 0-13-177334-8

Printed in the United States of America

Contents

Part 1: Human Origins and Human Cultures (5 million B.C.E. – 10,000 B.C.E.)

1. Humans had established themselves on all the continents of the earth except Antarctica by:
A. 15,000 B.C.E.
B. 5,000 B.C.E.
C. 15,000 C.E.
D. 250,000 B.C.E.

Ans: A
Diff: E
Page: 2

2. To better understand the prehistory of humans, historian must rely heavily upon:
A. Mythology
B. Archaeological evidence
C. Oral histories
D. Religious teachings

Ans: B
Diff: E
Page: 2

3. T F Until the mid-nineteenth century, questions about human origins were generally addressed by creation stories.

Ans: T
Diff: E
Page: 2

4. T F Human migration is motivated exclusively by the need to find food and shelter.

Ans: F
Diff: M
Page: 2

5. According to the text, what characteristics differentiate humans from other animals?

Difficulty: E
Page: 2

6. The cra in which village dwellers became adept at grinding and polishing stone tools is called the:
A. Paleolithic Age
B. Neolithic Age
C. Iron Age
D. Modern Age

Ans: B
Diff: E
Page: 37

7. Unlike most early village dwellers, the Jomon people in southern Japan supported themselves by:
A. cultivating rice
B. hunting, fishing and gathering
C. raiding supplies from neighboring villages
D. manufacturing and trading obsidian tools

Ans: B
Diff: M
Page: 39

8. T F Agricultural villages developed as population increases exceeded the ability of groups to safely and reliably procure sufficient food.

Ans: T
Diff: M
Page: 36

9. T F The villagers of Çatal Hüyük supported themselves by manufacturing and trading obsidian tools.

Ans: T
Diff: E
Page: 39

10. Explain the transition from hunting and gathering to village dwelling. What potential dangers or problems might transition create?

Diff: H
Pages: 36-38

Part 1: Human Origins and Human Cultures (5 million B.C.E. – 10,000 B.C.E.)
Chapter 1: The Dry Bones Speak (5 million B.C.E. – 10,000 B.C.E.)

1. Which of the following statements about the *Enuma Elish* is NOT true?
A. It probably dates to about 2000 B.C.E.
B. Humans were created by the gods out of earth and water
C. A rebelling god and goddess were destroyed by Marduk
D. It is the creation myth of the people of Akkad

Ans: B
Diff: M
Page: 5

2. The Purusa-sakta:
A. is a myth from Akkad culture
B. sets humans apart from nature
C. helped justify the caste system in India
D. holds that humans are not subject to the laws of the universe

Ans: C
Diff: M
Pages: 6-7

3. The book of Genesis holds that:
A. God created the world in seven days
B. God created man "in his own image"
C. humans are on an equal footing with animals
D. there are many gods worthy of worship

Ans: B
Diff: M
Page: 7

4. In the mid-1700s, the more astute natural scientists:
A. had developed the genetic theory of mutation transmission
B. had provided a substantial body of evidence that the Earth was many millions of years old
C. had proved the biblical account of creation
D. had questioned the idea that all plant and animal species had been separately created

Ans: D
Diff: M
Page: 7

5. Charles Darwin:
A. based his ideas on evolution on data he gathered while traveling in southeast Asia
B. refused to acknowledge that Alfred Russel Wallace had any useful ideas on evolution
C. acknowledged that there was a "Creator"
D. argued that teleology was an integral part of all life

Ans: C
Diff: M
Page: 9

6. T F According to Hindu thought, the questions about the origin of the world can be answered by observing nature.

Ans: F
Diff: H
Page: 6

7. T F According to the theory of natural selection, population pressure can affect the course of the evolution of a species.

Ans: T
Diff: M
Page: 9

8. T F By the early 1800s, archeological research had uncovered the definitive "missing link" between humans and apes.

Ans: F
Diff: M
Page: 10

9. Compare and contrast the creation myths presented in the text from India and the Hebrew Bible. How does each view the actual creation of the world and the status of humans in it?

Diff: M
Pages: 6-7

10. Present the main functions of creation myths.

Diff: M
Pages: 5-7

11. T F The use of fire by hominids can be traced to the Pleistocene period.

Ans: T
Diff: E
Page: 6

12. T F The cave paintings at Altamira were created by *Australopithecus*.

Ans: F
Diff: M
Page: 6

13. Fossil remains of the earliest direct human ancestors, *Australopithecus* and *Homo habilis*, have been found only in:
A. Australia
B. Asia
C. Africa
D. Western Europe

Ans: C
Diff: M
Page: 8

14. The remains of *Homo sapiens* have been found throughout:
A. Eurasia
B. Australia
C. Africa
D. Java

Ans: A
Diff: M
Page: 8

15. *Homo* first used fire about:
A. 5 million years ago
B. 1 million years ago
C. 200,000 years ago
D. 30,000 years ago

Ans: B
Diff: E
Page: 12

16. Louis and Mary Leakey selected the name *Homo habilis* because this hominid
A. had an unusually large jaw bone
B. utilized stone tools
C. possessed large, apelike teeth
D. had a very small skull

Ans: B
Diff: M
Page: 13

17. *Homo sapiens*:
A. means "man with developed brain"
B. were first discovered in fossils in the late seventeenth century
C. had the smallest brain capacity of any hominid yet discovered
D. was a tool user

Ans: D
Diff: M
Page: 15

18. Most archaeologists and paleoanthropologists believe:
A. *Homo erectus* first appeared in western Europe
B. *Homo erectus* first appeared in Africa
C. *Homo erectus* evolved into *Homo sapiens* only on the African continent
D. *Homo erectus* evolved into *Homo sapiens* in several regions

Ans: B
Diff: H
Page: 15

19. Regarding the hominid genetic record, it is NOT true that:
A. the significant study of the record began in the early 1950s
B. its study requires looking at the amount of similarity in the DNA of different hominids
C. study of mitochondrial DNA has led to controversial results
D. DNA studies have led some scientists to postulate that *Homo sapiens* emerged solely from Africa

Ans: A
Diff: M
Page: 19

20. T F In general, the farther back a hominid species is on the evolutionary "bush," the larger the average size of that species' brain capacity.

Ans: F
Diff: M
Page: 13

21. T F Most scientists agree that racial differences among modern humans had little to do with natural selection.

Ans: F
Diff: H
Page: 16

22. T F The debate over the "out-of-Africa" theory was finally resolved in 1970 due to DNA research.

Ans: F
Diff: M
Page: 19

23. Scientists disagree on the African origins of *Homo sapiens*. Describe the nature of the question, and then present the arguments of the two sides.

Diff: M
Pages: 15-18

24. According to Thomas Kuhn, how does science normally progress?

Diff: E
Page: 19

25. Which of the following events in evolutionary history happened first?
A. first dinosaurs
B. first reptiles
C. first amphibians
D. first birds

Ans: C
Diff: M
Page: 11

26. T F *Homo sapiens* was the product of interacting and interbreeding among a variety of earlier species.

Ans: T
Diff: E
Pages: 16-18

27. The "candelabra" model and the "Noah's Ark" model differ in their assessments of:
A. the geographic location of the evolution of *Homo sapiens*
B. the geographic origin of *Homo erectus*
C. the approximate date that *Homo erectus* left Africa
D. the approximate date of the first appearance of *Homo erectus*

Ans: A
Diff: H
Pages 15-16

28. *Homo sapiens*:
A. has not changed anatomically for at least 100,000 years
B. first appeared in the archaeological record about 400,000 years ago
C. did not coexist with Neanderthal man
D. did not create culture until near the end of the last ice age

Ans: A
Diff: M
Page: 21

29. Which of the following is NOT a reason put forth in the text for the disappearance of Neanderthals?
A. Neanderthals warred with each other and drove themselves to extinction
B. *Homo sapiens sapiens* destroyed the Neanderthals through violence
C. *Homo sapiens sapiens* out-competed Neanderthals for resources
D. Neanderthals interbred with *Homo sapiens sapiens*

Ans: A
Diff: M
Pages: 22-23

30. Global migration of *Homo sapiens sapiens*:
A. began around 450,000 B.C.E.
B. was often spurred by major climate changes
C. first occurred in the Americas
D. was usually random

Ans: B
Diff: M
Page: 24

31. Linguist Noam Chomsky argues that the ability to use language is:
A. learned from parents
B. learned from the environment
C. genetic
D. a gift of the gods

Ans: C
Diff: M
Page: 29

32. The "Venus" figurine pictured in the text:
A. was made between 5,000 and 7,000 years ago
B. indicates that the people of that era were on a near-starvation diet
C. is probably a fertility charm
D. was found in southern Africa

Ans: C
Diff: E
Page: 30

33. T F *Homo sapiens* females are capable of bearing more children than other primates.

Ans: T
Diff: E
Page: 20

34. T F Scientists have a good idea of when *Homo* developed speech.

Ans: F
Diff: M
Page: 29

35. T F The earliest farmers probably engaged in agriculture in part because they felt it was the most efficient way to gain food.

Ans: T
Diff: M
Page: 32

36. What was the major reason behind the global migration of *Homo sapiens sapiens*? How does this tie in to Darwin's theory of evolution?

Diff: M
Pages: 23-24

37. Why was the development of modern language so significant to human development?

Diff: M
Page: 29

38. Which of the following stages of human development happened first?
A. domestication of animals
B. human migrations to America
C. development of speech
D. rapid brain growth

Ans: D
Diff: M
Page: 21

39. Explain the differences between radiocarbon dating and thermoluminescence, and give an example to illustrate the most useful application of each method.

Diff: H
Page: 22

40. Describe the relationship between the Ice Age and the global migration of humans.

Diff: M
Pages: 23-24

41. Of the following regions, which was the last colonized by *Homo sapiens sapiens*?
A. Africa
B. Polynesia
C. Asia
D. South America

Ans: B
Diff: E
Page: 24

42. Anthropologist Sally Slocum:
A. waited until the 1990s to present her feminist critique of anthropology
B. thinks that answers are what is important, not the questions the answers are based on
C. stresses the prime importance of gathering in the evolution of hominids
D. thought that hunting was of no significant relevance to hominid evolution

Ans: C
Diff: H
Page: 26

43. T F Over time, human stone tools became more sophisticated.

Ans: T
Diff: E
Page: 27

Part 2: Settling Down (10,000 B.C.E. – 1000 C.E.)

1. When the first cities developed, most of the world's population was:
A. farmers or merchants
B. raiders or hunter-gatherers
C. hunter-gathers or farmers
D. farmers or raiders

Ans: C
Diff: E
Page: 41

2. The world's earliest cities developed:
A. in fertile Plains regions
B. along major river systems
C. exclusively along coastal waters
D. around large manufacturing facilities

Ans: B
Diff: M
Page: 41

3. T F Until the late nineteenth century, most people did NOT live in an urban environment.

Ans: T
Diff: M
Page: 41

4. T F Of all the major Mesopotamian cities, only Ur contained a ziggurat dedicated to a deity.

Ans: F
Diff: E
Page: 41

5. Explain the connection between spiritual beliefs and early cities.

Difficulty: M
Page: 41

6. The first recorded empire in history was created in:
A. Egypt
B. Mesopotamia
C. West Africa
D. the Indus valley

Ans: B
Diff: E
Page: 118

7. Sargon of Akkad succeeded in creating an empire due to his:
A. superior weapons technology
B. opponents' failure to protect their cities with fortifications
C. advantage in numbers, organization, skill and energy
D. opponents' lack of an organized army

Ans: C
Diff: M
Page: 118

8. T F New immigrant groups introduced two-wheeled chariots and bronze-tipped arrows into the Fertile Crescent region by about 1500 B.C.E.

Ans: T
Diff: E
Pages: 119-120

9. T F The Persians invented the crossbow in the tenth-century C.E.

Ans: F
Diff: M
Page: 120

10. Which of the following was used as one of the earliest and most common psychological weapons?
A. horse-drawn chariots
B. sound instruments
C. flaming, bronze-tipped arrows
D. ceramic soldiers

Ans: B
Diff: M
Page: 121

11. In addition to military prowess, what other skills and knowledge are essential to the development of an empire?

Diff: H
Page: 121

1. The Neolithic Age:
A. preceded the Paleolithic Age
B. is named for the characteristics of its tools
C. began substantially prior to the founding of the first cities
D. was a time in which trade was virtually nonexistent

Ans: B
Diff: M
Page: 45

2. The first animals to be domesticated in the "Fertile Crescent" were:
A. goats and sheep
B. pigs and cattle
C. dogs
D. llamas and turkeys

Ans: A
Diff: E
Page: 45

3. The use of ceramics is usually an indicator that the owners were:
A. nomadic
B. village dwellers
C. relatively unskilled
D. traders

Ans: B
Diff: M
Page: 45

4. The earliest staple crops in central India included:
A. yams
B. gourds
C. rice
D. legumes

Ans: C
Diff: M
Page: 45

5. The distinctive characteristics of Neolithic pottery include:
A. the lack of decorative features
B. fine designs and colors
C. simplistic, geometric designs
D. the lack of vibrant colors

Ans: B
Diff: M
Page: 45

6. T F Ceramics are never found among nomadic populations.

Ans: F
Diff: E
Page: 45

7. T F In addition to fishing, the Jomon villagers of Japan hunted gazelles

Ans: F
Diff: E
Page: 46

8. T F The Japanese did NOT develop agricultural cultivation until several thousand years after they began to live in villages

Ans: T
Diff: E
Page: 46

9. Compare and contrast the toolkit used by hunter-gatherers with that used by farmers.

Diff: M
Page: 45

10. Describe the connection between the physical environment and the development of the first villages.

Diff: M
Pages: 44-45

11. Which of the following empires was organized first?
A. Persian
B. Hittite
C. Neo-Babylonian
D. Assyrian

Ans: B
Diff: E
Page: 44

12. Of the following, which is located farthest from the Fertile Crescent?
A. Tigris River
B. Red Sea
C. Mediterranean Sea
D. western Iranian plateau

Ans: D
Diff: M
Page: 45

13. T F Horses were first domesticated in China.

Ans: F
Diff. M
Page: 46

14. Most experts think that innovative primary urbanization:
A. could not have happened without diffusive urbanization
B. occurred only in the fertile crescent
C. occurred only in Asia
D. must have begun after the practice of agriculture

Ans: D
Diff: H
Page: 46

15. Urbanization began latest:
A. in Mesopotamia
B. along the Nile River
C. along the Indus River
D. along the Niger River

Ans: D
Diff: M
Page: 47

16. The Bronze Age:
A. preceded the Paleolithic Age
B. was a time of significant technological breakthroughs
C. was a time when little of relevance occurred
D. occurred before there were written records

Ans: B
Diff: E
Page: 47

17. As cities became more developed:
A. new class hierarchies emerged
B. the need for armies diminished
C. decision making became much more egalitarian
D. contact with other communities became less common

Ans: A
Diff: M
Page: 47

18. The world's first system of writing evolved in:
A. the Indus Valley
B. southeast Asia
C. Sumer
D. Khmer

Ans: C
Diff: E
Page: 48

19. T F The earliest cities evolved along major river systems as a result of diffusion rather than innovation.

Ans: F
Diff: M
Page: 46

20. T F As cities became larger, their organization became more complex.

Ans: T
Diff: E
Page: 47

21. T F In the Andes, record keeping was initially accomplished through the use of tokens and pictures.

Ans: F
Diff: M
Page: 48

22. Explain the difference between innovation and diffusion in the development of urban centers.

Diff: M
Page: 46

23. Explain why written language was one of the most revolutionary inventions in human history.

Diff: M
Page: 48

24. T F Most of the earliest civilizations developed in the northern hemisphere.

Ans: T
Diff: M
Page: 47

25. Which region witnessed the earliest urban settlement?
A. sub-Saharan Africa
B. southern Mesopotamia
C. Mesoamerica
D. the Indus plain.

Ans: B
Diff: E
Page: 47

26. The Sumerians:
A. originally came from Northern Africa
B. were eventually displaced by the Ubaid peoples
C. dominated Mesopotamia for nearly a millennium
D. were eventually conquered by Alexander the Great

Ans: C
Diff: M
Pages: 48-49

27. The Sumerians were finally conquered by:
A. Sargon of Akkad
B. Nefertiti of Egypt
C. Alexander the Great of Macedon
D. Hammurabi of Babylon

Ans: D
Diff: M
Page: 49

28. Although the Sumerians did not speak Semitic, their use of Semitic names suggests:
A. that they had migrated from a Semitic speaking region
B. Semitic-speaking people may have preceded them in the area
C. their language had evolved from Semitic
D. they had been ruled at one time by a Semitic-speaking people

Ans: B
Diff: M
Page: 48

29. Which of the following is NOT a Sumerian city-state?
A. Kish
B. Uruk
C. Akkad
D. Lagash

Ans: C
Diff: M
Page: 49

30. The city-states of Mesopotamia were especially vulnerable due to:
A. inter-urban warfare
B. powerful external enemies
C. their lack of organized armies
D. inability to grow enough food to adequately feed their populations

Ans: A
Diff: M
Page: 49

31. T F The city-states of Sumer cooperated peacefully to ensure the economic success of the region.

Ans: F
Diff: E
Page: 48

32. T F The cities of Sumer were ruled for about 200 years by Sargon, the king of Akkad.

Ans: T
Diff: E
Page: 49

33. T F The Sumerian city-states are notable for their lack of religious meeting places.

Ans: F
Diff: M
Page: 48

34. Describe how the Sumerians were able to build long-standing cities in a region subject to unpredictable flooding.

Diff: M
Page: 48

35. Explain how the Sumerian cities were able to provide enough food to meet the needs of the cities' growing populations.

Diff: M
Page: 48

36. In Sumerian times, the idea of legal identity and loyalty was based most fundamentally on:
A. religion
B. class
C. geography
D. clan

Ans: C
Diff: M
Page: 50

37. In Sumer after about 2800 B.C.E., members of this group ruled in conjunction with kings:
A. temple priests
B. large landowners
C. rich artisans
D. peasants' representatives

Ans: A
Diff: E
Pages: 50-51

38. Sumerian trade:
A. relied entirely on donkey caravan
B. never made significant use of the boat
C. extended as far as the Indus valley
D. primarily involved trading surplus Sumerian foodstuffs and products for gold and silver

Ans: C
Diff: E
Page: 53

39. Which type of writing occurred first?
A. pictographic writing
B. Assyrian writing
C. phonetic writing
D. cuneiform writing

Ans: A
Diff: E
Page: 55

40. Sumerian cuneiform writing was displaced primarily due to the actions of:
A. Alexander the Great
B. Hammurabi
C. Jewish immigrants entering the Mesopotamian region around 1,000 B.C.E.
D. the Hittites

Ans: A
Diff: M
Page: 55

41. T F Most people used in human sacrifice in Sumer were slaves.

Ans: F
Diff: M
Page: 51

42. T F One significant result of metallurgy was the creation of more effective weapons.

Ans: T
Diff: M
Page: 53

43. T F Gilgamesh was the legendary ruler of the Sumerian city Uruk.

Ans: T
Diff: E
Page: 56

44. Describe the Sumerian priesthood and ziggurats. How much power did the priesthood have? How did it maintain its power?

Diff: M
Page: 51

45. Many believe that the agricultural village was more peaceful and more egalitarian than the first cities? Is this true? Support your answer.

Diff: M
Page: 61

46. T F The Sumerian trading network extended as far west as modern day Afghanistan.

Ans: T
Diff: M
Page: 52

47. T F Alphabetic writing preceded the development of cuneiform.

Ans: F
Diff: E
Page: 55

48. Of the following, which has given us the best idea of important Sumerian values?
A. king lists
B. royal correspondence
C. lamentations
D. epics

Ans: D
Diff: H
Page: 56

49. Enkidu's attraction to the city most fundamentally illustrates the:
A. decline in importance of the natural world relative to that of the city
B. weakness of religion in Sumerian society
C. irresistible lure of politics
D. value Sumerians placed on friendship

Ans: A
Diff: H
Page: 57

50. This people invented writing:
A. Egyptians
B. Akkadians
C. Babylonians
D. Sumerians

Ans: D
Diff: E
Page: 58

51. Compare the probable rights and powers of women in the typical pre-urban village with those of women living in the typical urban Sumerian city. Did the establishment of cities help women overall, or did it hurt them? Explain

Diff: H
Page: 59

52. Describe the class structure of the typical Sumerian city. Where did the preponderance of power lie? Did the class structure agree with Marxist analysis?

Diff: H
Page: 60

1. Scholars know the least about this civilization:
A. Greek city-states
B. Indus valley
C. Nile valley
D. Tigris-Euphrates valley

Ans: B
Diff: E
Page: 65

2. We know less about ancient Egyptian cities when compared with ancient Mesopotamian cities primarily because the Egyptian cities were:
A. destroyed by war
B. few and far between
C. destroyed by the Nile River
D. changed so drastically by the British in the nineteenth and twentieth centuries

Ans: C
Diff: M
Page: 66

3. The economies of the villages that developed along the Nile River were based on:
A. commercial trade
B. cereal agriculture
C. fishing
D. warfare

Ans: B
Diff: E
Page: 66

4. Egyptians wrote on paper made from:
A. limestone flakes
B. linen
C. papyrus pith
D. cotton

Ans: C
Diff: E
Page: 67

5. The earliest known writing samples were concerned primarily with:
A. commerce
B. the activities of royalty
C. religious practices
D. law codes

Ans: A
Diff: E
Page: 67

6. T F Written records for ancient Egypt enabled scholars to learn more about the Egyptian state than almost any other.

Ans: T
Diff: E
Page: 66

7. T F Egyptian writing began nearly a thousand years before Mesopotamian writing.

Ans: F
Diff: M
Page: 67

8. T F The earliest Egyptian records reveal a list of the early kings dating back as early as 2900 B.C.E.

Ans: T
Diff: E
Page: 67

9. Describe the relationship between the Nile River and the development of Egyptian cities.

Diff: E
Page: 66

10. Explain the evidence used by scholars to support their claim that by 3300 B.C.E. there were new levels of social stratification in Upper Egypt.

Diff: M
Page: 67

11. The Rosetta Stone:
A. was discovered by an expedition led by Richelieu
B. was found in the Valley of the Kings in southern Egypt
C. contains three types of writing
D. did not have its significance recognized until the mid-twentieth century

Ans: C
Diff: M
Page: 68

12. Horus:
A. became the main god of the pharaohs
B. was the father of Osiris
C. ruled the underworld
D. represented the southern portion of Egypt

Ans: A
Diff: M
Page: 69

13. Hierakonpolis:
A. experienced its greatest growth during a time of ecological balance
B. was a herald of the coming "Nagada II" culture
C. disposed of its dead in the Nile
D. was on the Mediterranean Sea near the mouth of the Nile

Ans: B
Diff: H
Page: 72

14. Most of the great Egyptian pyramids were built:
A. after Egypt was conquered by Persia
B. during the Old Kingdom
C. just before the Third Intermediate Period
D. after the region converted to Islam

Ans: B
Diff: M
Page: 74

15. Akhetaten:
A. was built by the pharaoh Ramses II
B. is considered the best representative of the typical Egyptian city of its day
C. was used as a capital for nearly 800 years
D. was the site of worship of the sun god Aten

Ans: D
Diff: M
Page: 78

16. T F After 3100 B.C.E., Egyptians, Semites, Phoenicians, Blacks, and Europeans intermarried in Egypt without apparent references to race or ethnicity.

Ans: T
Diff: E
Page: 68

17. T F The Old Kingdom fell in 2181 B.C.E. as the result of a hostile attack by King Mentuhotpe of Thebes.

Ans: F
Diff: M
Pages: 76-77

18. T F The Middle Kingdom ended in part due to invasions of the Hyksos who probably came from north and east of the Sinai desert.

Ans: T
Diff: M
Page: 78

19. Describe the power of the pharaohs that ordered the construction of the Great Pyramids. Also discuss what the pyramids represented.

Diff: E
Pages: 74-75

20. The powers of the pharaohs changed substantially over time, often from one pharaoh to another depending upon abilities and outside factors. With this in mind, write an essay discussing and analyzing the decline of the Old Kingdom and the rise of the Middle Kingdom.

Diff: H
Page: 78

21. T F The power of Egyptian kings increased until they became accepted as gods around 3000 B.C.E.

Ans: T
Diff: E
Page: 66

22. In ancient Egypt:
A. the Red Sea was to the north
B. Upper Egypt was to the north
C. Nubia was to the south
D. most pyramids were located near the fifth cataract

Ans: C
Diff: E
Page: 67

23. What is the significance of the Rosetta Stone for Egyptology?

Diff: E
Page: 69

24. T F Amenhotep worshipped many gods.

Ans: F
Diff: E
Page: 70

25. Describe the purpose of the Egyptian *Book of the Dead*.

Diff: M
Page: 76

26. Explain the purpose of the *Autobiography of Si-nuhe*. Why is it prized as the "crown jewel of Middle Egyptian literature"?

Diff: M
Page: 77

27. The early twentieth century excavations of the Harappan civilization in the Indus valley reveal that it likely:
A. was originated by Aryan immigrants from Persia
B. began around 4500 B.C.E.
C. developed independently from civilizations in Mesopotamia
D. had many small towns, but no cities

Ans: C
Diff: M
Page: 80

28. The Harappan civilization:
A. was centered on one large city: Harappa
B. had a strong central government
C. was based along the Ganges river
D. had a language, but it has not yet been deciphered

Ans: D
Diff: E
Page: 80

29. The art and craftwork of the Indus Valley indicates:
A. that the civilization was not very well developed
B. they participated in active interregional trade
C. they did not possess metallurgical skills
D. they were a nomadic people

Ans: B
Diff: E
Page: 80

30. The settlements of Harrapa and Mohenjo-Daro could each accommodate:
A. about 40,000 residents
B. about 2,500 residents
C. about 10,000 residents
D. about 25,000 residents

Ans: A
Diff: E
Page: 81

31. Which of the following is NOT one of the four legacies of Harappa described in the text?
A. Aryan invaders adopted some of the settlement characteristics of the Indus valley civilization
B. Aryan invaders adopted some of the Indus valley agricultural techniques
C. Aryan invaders nearly completely destroyed the Indus valley civilization
D. Aryan invaders may have adopted some religious ideas of the Indus valley civilization

Ans: C
Diff: M
Pages: 83-84

32. T F The study of the Indus valley civilization began in earnest in the first half of the twentieth century.

Ans: T
Diff: E
Page: 79

33. T F Archeological evidence reveals the mutual trade of goods between the Indus valley and Mesopotamia.

Ans: T
Diff: M
Page: 80

34. T F The Indus valley had numerous cities and a clearly defined state political system connecting them.

Ans: F
Diff: E
Page: 83

35. Describe the important aspects of how modern archaeologists and historians discovered and investigated the Indus valley civilization. Include in your essay a discussion of the important characteristics of that civilization.

Diff: H
Pages: 79-80

36. What do we know about the class structure and eventual decline of the Indus valley civilization? Do scholars agree? If not, what are the contending hypotheses?

Diff: H
Pages: 83-84

37. The Indus valley civilization:
A. began around 7000 B.C.E.
B. reached its apex around 1000 B.C.E.
C. made little use of agricultural practices
D. built numerous temples and palaces

Ans: A
Diff: M
Page: 79

38. T F Major Harrapan sites are found exclusively along the coast of the Arabian Sea.

Ans: F
Diff: E
Page: 81

39. T F Excavations of Mohenjo-Daro reveal that the city was serviced by an underground sewerage and drainage system.

Ans: T
Diff: E
Page: 81

40. The use of iron occurred:
A. before the use of the plow and cart
B. after the use of bronze
C. before the use of pottery
D. after the time of Christ

Ans: B
Diff: E
Page: 83

41. Which of the many theories concerning the decline of the Indus civilization do you find most convincing? Explain your reasoning.

Diff: M
Page: 84

1. Neolithic groups in China began the transition from hunting and gathering to farming and village life as early as:
A. 1700 B.C.E.
B. 9000 B.C.E.
C. 8000 B.C.E.
D. 2700 B.C.E.

Ans: C
Diff: E
Page: 89

2. China's three earliest known dynasties:
A. were centered on the Yangzi River
B. were each at one time the most powerful regional dynasty
C. did not overlap each other
D. showed a reverential respect for the sanctity of human life

Ans: B
Diff: M
Page: 91

3. Chinese oracle bones:
A. have been useful to archaeologists, anthropologists, and historians for at least three centuries
B. first came to the attention of scientists after they were found at excavation sites
C. have provided useful information about the rulers of the Shang dynasty
D. were usually made from human bones

Ans: C
Diff: M
Pages: 91-92

4. The Xia dynasty:
A. apparently did not make pottery
B. was ruled by a single king who controlled all the powers of the state
C. did not leave any significant archaeological sites, so little is known about it
D. had rulers that engaged in rituals and divinations

Ans: D
Diff: H
Page: 93

5. The Shang state was characterized by a:
A. king who allowed relatives to rule regional areas
B. loose network of independent towns and cities
C. leader who traveled from city to city, with no set capital
D. time of little warfare

Ans: A
Diff: M
Page: 94

6. Anyang:
A. was the last capital of the Zhou dynasty
B. was the center of a small empire about 30 miles in diameter
C. is one of the most extensively investigated archaeological sites in China
D. was mentioned in Shang texts, though it was referred to by a different name

Ans: D
Diff: H
Page: 95

7. T F The Xia, Shang and Zhou dynasties were all located around the Huang He (Yellow River) valley.

Ans: T
Diff: E
Page: 90

8. T F Unlike the Shang and Zhou dynasties, the Xia did NOT build walled towns.

Ans: F
Diff: M
Page: 93

9. T F There is some evidence that women could wield power in the earliest Chinese dynasties.

Ans: T
Diff: E
Page: 93

10 T F The capital of the Shang dynasty was permanently located at Anyang.

Ans: F
Diff: E
Page: 95

11. Describe the discoveries that convinced historians that the Xia and Shang dynasties were more than just legends.

Diff: M
Pages: 92-93

12. Explain the modifications implemented by the Zhou dynasty to enable it to control a much larger state than that ruled by the Shang dynasty?

Diff: M
Page: 97

13. Which of the following innovations was developed first?
A. the crossbow
B. Longshan ceramics
C. farming with domesticated animals
D. Yangshao penal code

Ans: D
Diff: M
Page: 90

14. T F The Longshan culture extended further west than the Shang culture.

15. Which of the following was the more recent development in early Chinese culture?
A. domestication of the water buffalo
B. primitive writing
C. domestication of the horse
D. human grave sacrifices

16. Describe how modern investigators of early Chinese history used texts, oracle bones and archaeological techniques to gain information.

17. Explain how the Zhou poem, "Pivot of the Four Quarters" supports the theory that ancient Chinese cities developed from ritual centers.

18. The first cities of the Americas:
A. began as trade centers
B. never developed into city-states
C. were linked to the other-world through shamans
D. were located along major rivers

19. What did the first cities in the Americas have in common with the first cities of Asia?
A. use of pack animals
B. use of the wheel
C. use of metal tools
D. use of draft animals

20. The Teotihuacán civilization:
A. flourished on the coast of the Gulf of Mexico
B. was destroyed by the Spanish conquistadors
C. never expanded more than a few miles beyond the borders of the city
D. built the Pyramid of the Sun

21. Tikal:
A. is located near present-day Mexico City
B. was notable for its lack of pyramids
C. extended its influence well beyond the city boundaries
D. flourished until it was destroyed by the Spanish

Ans: C
Diff: M
Page: 104

22. Early urbanization in South America:
A. was spurred by the high volume of trade with Mesoamerica
B. followed a much different path than that typical in Mesoamerica
C. centered on religious shrines
D. was not significant until about 500 C.E.

Ans: C
Diff: H
Page: 106

23. The Inca empire:
A. lasted for nearly 1000 years
B. practiced monotheism
C. built an extensive network of roads and paths
D. forbade any use of the religion or culture of its predecessor states

Ans: C
Diff: M
Page: 110

24. The agricultural settlements found in North America around 1200 C.E. are not usually considered sites of primary urbanization because:
A. they better fit the model of tertiary urbanization
B. they were too far north of Mesoamerica
C. their populations were too low
D. they cultivated only one crop

Ans: C
Diff: M
Page: 111

25. T F By 5000 B.C.E., the early inhabitants of the Americas were cultivating maize.

Ans: T
Diff: E
Page: 98

26. T F The Toltec, Aztec, and Maya repudiated all aspects of the Teotihuácan civilization.

Ans: F
Diff: M
Page: 102

27. T F The quality and designs of the textiles produced in coastal Peru rivaled those produced in the Indus valley.

Ans: T
Diff: M
Page: 108

28. T F The artwork of the Hohokam people in North America illustrates that they were influenced by Mexican and South American designs.

Ans: T
Diff: E
Page: 111

29. Describe the major characteristics of pre-Columbian urban development in South America in both coastal and mountain areas. Which civilization was the most advanced?

Diff: H
Pages: 107-108

30. Discuss how the Inca Empire formed and how it organized society, religion, and government.

Diff: M
Page: 110

31. T F The Maya civilization predated the Toltec civilization.

Ans: T
Diff: E
Page: 97

32. T F The most impressive civilizations in South America were located along the Pacific Coast.

Ans: F
Diff: M
Page: 99

33. T F The city of Teotihuácan was organized on a regular grid pattern.

Ans: T
Diff: E
Page: 101

34. The *Popol Vuh* contains the creation myth of the:
A. Roman Catholic conquistadores from Spain
B. the Inca civilization
C. the Mayan civilization
D. the Aztec civilization

Ans: C
Diff: E
Page: 105

35. What does the Tikal stelae tell us about the military power of the Mayan civilization?

Diff: M
Page: 106

36. Describe how the decoding of the Mayan language in the 1970s transformed our understanding of the Mayan civilization. What "new" evidence did this reveal?

Diff: M
Page: 107

37. Which of the following Central American civilizations was the first to develop sophisticated astronomy?
A. Aztec
B. Teotihuácan
C. Olmec
D. Mayan

Ans: D
Diff: M
Page: 108

38. The South American civilization known for its enormous "geoglyphs," best seen in an aerial view is:
A. the Huari
B. the Inca
C. the Nazca
D. the Tiwanaka

Ans: C
Diff: M
Page: 109

39. Iron smelting in West Africa:
A. took place after urbanization had progressed substantially
B. developed gradually
C. began around 200 C.E.
D. was introduced from outside the region

Ans: D
Diff: M
Page: 112

40. The Bantu:
A. only settled regions far south of the Niger River
B. never did practice agriculture
C. migrated thousands of miles to southern Africa
D. were well-known for their copper-shaping skills

Ans: C
Diff: E
Pages: 112-113

41. Of the following African cities, which one is NOT believed to have followed a development pattern introduced from other cultures?
A. Jenne-Jeno
B. Kush
C. Aksum
D. Malindi

Ans: A
Diff: E
Page: 113

42. Jenne-Jeno:
A. was first excavated in the early twentieth century
B. was a settlement on the Yellow River
C. did not appear to engage in trade
D. was founded around 250 B.C.E.

Ans: D
Diff: M
Page: 113

43. In the Niger River valley, the primary urban settlement that has been excavated suggests:
A. that cities may develop without the need for hierarchy, centralization, government structure, or written language
B. the development of cities is contingent upon the development of a centralized political authority
C. written language is fundamental for the organization of an urban center
D. cities cannot develop without the pre-existence of hierarchical social organization

Ans: A
Diff: M
Page: 115

44. T F The Bantu spread their language and metallurgical skills throughout Africa by 500 C.E.

Ans: T
Diff: E
Page: 113

45. T F The people of Jenne-jeno enjoyed a varied diet of fish, rice, beef and milk.

Ans: T
Diff: E
Page: 113

46. T F Archaeological evidence uncovered at Jenne-jeno indicates that they did NOT practice ancestor worship.

Ans: F
Diff: M
Page: 113

47. In what ways did the Bantu culture have a major affect on Africa?

Diff: E
Page: 112

48. Discuss the discovery of Jenne-jeno and what is currently known about its nature and the practices of the people who inhabited it.

Diff: M
Page: 113

49. T F Cities were observed in the Niger valley more than 700 years before the founding of the Kingdom of Mali.

Ans: T
Diff: M
Page: 111

50. T F Extensive trade routes connected the West African state of Ghana with both Egypt and Tunisia.

Ans: T
Diff: E
Page: 112

51. The impact of the Bantu culture can be seen in which of the following regions:
A. Egypt
B. the Saharan Desert
C. the Kalahari Desert
D. Madagascar

Ans: C
Diff: E
Page: 113

1. Which of the following constitutes the first example of empire building?
A. Persia
B. Egypt
C. Akkad
D. Greece

Ans: C
Diff: E
Page: 122

2. Against which of the following did the Greeks successfully resist in the fifth century B.C.E.?
A. Persia
B. Egypt
C. China
D. Japan

Ans: A
Diff: M
Page: 122

3. T F It can be argued that the Roman empire endured for approximately 2000 years.

Ans: T
Diff: M
Page: 123

4. T F Ashok Maurya, who came to power in the Indian subcontinent in 273 B.C.E, is no longer included in Indian history books.

Ans: F
Diff: M
Page: 123

5. Describe the life-cycle or pattern of empire that emerged in Mesopotamia, the Nile Valley and the Yellow River valley.

Diff: M
Page: 122

6. The Bhagavad Gita is the revered text of which religious group?
A. Buddhists
B. Hindus
C. Christians
D. Muslims

Ans: B
Diff: E
Page: 266

7. The teachings of Buddha were spread throughout Asia under orders from
A. Gilgamesh
B. Muhammad
C. Moses
D. Asoka

Ans: D
Diff: E
Page: 267

8. T F In the ancient world, there was no distinction made between religious leaders and political rulers.

Ans: F
Diff: M
Page: 264

9. T F Muhammad's teachings were NOT accepted as authoritative until he assumed political leadership of Medina.

Ans: T
Diff: E
Page: 266

10. Does acceptance by political leaders foster or impede the dissemination of religious ideas? Explain the relationship.

Diff: M
Pages: 266-267

1. Empires:
A. usually grow through conquest
B. by definition share rule with conquered peoples
C. have been few and far between in human history over the last five millennia
D. exist primarily to enrich conquered areas

Ans: A
Diff: E
Page: 125

2. The phrase "All roads lead to Rome," refers to:
A. the extensive construction of roads by the Romans as they expanded their empire
B. the concept that exotic goods and diverse peoples were all brought together under the centralized rule of Rome.
C. the lack of a developed transportation network leading to destinations other than Rome
D. that all imperial subjects must make a trip to Rome once in their lifetimes.

Ans: B
Diff: M
Page: 125

3. Imperial dominance:
A. has little effect on the likelihood of revolt by subjugated peoples
B. exists when rulers make no attempt to gain the allegiance of conquered peoples
C. requires the use of sheer power to enforce rule
D. is another term for imperial hegemony

Ans: C
Diff: M
Page: 126

4. Usually the most important administrative function of an empire is to:
A. provide uniformity of language to ensure good communication with conquered peoples
B. efficiently collect taxes from all peoples in the empire
C. enforce a just and comprehensive legal code
D. create and enforce a good system of weights and measures

Ans: B
Diff: H
Page: 126

5. Of the following, which is NOT a major cause of the decline and fall of empires?
A. overextension of the administration
B. fanatical belief in the ideology of the empire
C. economic collapse
D. failure of leadership

Ans: B
Diff: M
Pages: 126-127

6. T F Conquered peoples in an empire are less likely to revolt if hegemony exists rather than dominance.

Ans: T
Diff: H
Page: 126

7. T F For the conquered population, imperial hegemony offers no benefits.

Ans: F
Diff: M
Page: 126

8. T F The collapse of an empire is always preceded by war with a competing imperial power.

Ans: F
Diff: M
Pages: 126-127

9. Exactly what is an empire? How does it grow? What are the typical functions performed by an empire, and what are the main causes that typically lead to an empire's decline and demise?

Diff: H
Pages: 125-127

10. Describe the five main reasons the text gives for the decline and fall of empires.

Diff: E
Pages: 126-127

11. Mesopotamia's earliest power centers:
A. usually were able to reach accommodation with each other through peaceful means
B. were centered on Nineveh and Yarmuti
C. contented themselves with their borders
D. often fought over land and irrigation rights

Ans: D
Diff: M
Page: 127

12. The Akkadian empire:
A. reached its greatest height under Hammurabi
B. was led by Elamites
C. lasted for nearly six centuries
D. connected Mesopotamia to the eastern Mediterranean coast

Ans: D
Diff: M
Page: 127

13. The Hittite empire was centered in:
A. Mesopotamia
B. Palestine
C. the upper Nile
D. Anatolia

Ans: D
Diff: E
Page: 129

14. The Assyrians:
A. were descendants of the Hittites
B. asserted their empire on three separate occasions
C. never managed to extend their empire to the Mediterranean
D. failed in their bid to conquer Egypt

Ans: B
Diff: H
Page: 130

15. Ancient Egypt:
A. was often a unified state
B. was quite vulnerable to attack from the south
C. was quite vulnerable to attack from the west
D. was quite vulnerable to attack from the east

Ans: A
Diff: M
Page: 131

16. T F The Amorites were a Hittite group that conquered Sumer and founded their own dynasty at Babylon.

Ans: F
Diff: M
Page: 128

17. T F The city-state organization of Mesopotamia made them invulnerable to attack

Ans: F
Diff: E
Page: 130

18. T F When Nubia successfully rebelled against Egypt, they reversed the long-standing relationship between colonizer and colonized.

Ans: T
Diff: M
Page: 134

19. Describe the factors that contributed to the decline of the Mesopotamian empire.

Diff: M
Page: 130

20. Describe the international conquests of the Egyptians, including a description of the greatest extent of its borders.

Diff: M
Page: 134

21. Under Sargon, the Mesopotamian empire connected which of the following bodies of water?
A. the Black Sea and the Caspian Sea
B. the Caspian Sea and the Persian Gulf
C. the Persian Gulf and the Mediterranean Sea
D. the Mediterranean Sea and the Black Sea

Ans: C
Diff: E
Page: 127

22. T F By 650 B.C.E., the Assyrian Empire included Egypt.

Ans: T
Diff: E
Page: 129

23. T F Egyptian civilization did NOT extend beyond the second cataract.

Ans: F
Diff: E
Page: 130

24. Which of the following was at different times controlled by the Hittites and by the Mitanni?
A. Tarsus
B. Babylon
C. Harran
D. Nineveh

Ans: C
Diff: M
Page: 133

25. The balance of power among the Egyptians, Medes, Babylonians, and Lydians was broken by
A. Cyrus II
B. Cambyses I
C. Cambyses II
D. Darius I

Ans: A
Diff: E
Page: 134

26. Which Persian ruler was the least benevolent to his subjects?
A. Cambyses II
B. Cyrus II
C. Darius I
D. Alexander the Great

Ans: A
Diff: M
Page: 137

27. Darius I:
A. was the son of Cyrus the Great
B. enforced a Persian legal code throughout his empire
C. did not attempt to collect taxes from most of the conquered areas
D. allowed a large measure of local control over administration and religion within his empire

Ans: D
Diff: M
Page: 139

28. Our understanding of Persian artistic design is based primarily on:
A. the paintings found in Persepolis
B. the imperial architecture of Persepolis
C. the iron-work wall that surrounds the city of Persepolis
D. the sculptures uncovered from the ruins of Persepolis

Ans: B
Diff: M
Page: 138

29. The teachings of Zoroastrianism spread under the rule of which of the following?
A. Cyrus I
B.Cambyses II
C. Darius I
D. Cyrus II

Ans: C
Diff: E
Page: 139

30. T F The legends surrounding the exploits of Cyrus II were so great that the Babylonians allowed him to capture the city without putting up a fight

Ans: T
Diff: E
Page: 135

31. T F Under the authority of Darius I, the Persian Empire extended all the way to the Bay of Bengal

Ans: F
Diff: M
Page: 135

32. T F Under the leadership of Cambyses II, the Persian Empire secured its greatest territorial and financial success

Ans: F
Diff: M
Page: 137

33. Explain the actions taken by Darius I to ensure the continued economic success of the region.

Diff: H
Page: 138

34. Describe the administrative policies of Cyrus the Great and Darius I. How much freedom did they allow their subjects? Do you think some of the subjects welcomed the opportunity to be part of the Persian Empire?

Diff: H
Pages: 136-139

Charts/Graphs/Maps/Boxed Features

35. During the reign of Cyrus II, the Royal Road of the Persian Empire connected which of the following cities?
A. Athens and Kandahar
B. Memphis and Babylon
C. Byzantium and Persepolis
D. Sardis and Susa

Ans: D
Diff: M
Page: 135

36. Crete:
A. has, because of its location, never been a significant trade center
B. was once controlled by Mycenae
C. was the home of Troy
D. was first settled in about 1400 B.C.E.

Ans: B
Diff: E
Page: 141

37. The Greek city-state:
A. had political powers analogous to that of a state within the United States
B. was kept small by wars with the Persian empire
C. typically had populations exceeding 100,000
D. usually centered on a single city

Ans: D
Diff: E
Page: 141

38. Solon:
A. instituted a law providing for debtors' prisons
B. relied on the hereditary aristocracy for power
C. allowed common people to have an impact on government
D. had his important reforms last for nearly two centuries after his death

Ans: C
Diff: M
Page: 143

39. The use of the deme in Greek city-state politics made political identity dependent upon:
A. geography
B. ideology
C. religion
D. socioeconomic class

Ans: A
Diff: M
Page: 144

40. The Persian Empire:
A. maintained itself through a balance of power among the major Middle East states
B. reached its greatest geographical extent under Cyrus the Great
C. failed to defeat Greece at the battle of Marathon
D. easily conquered the Scythians

Ans: C
Diff: M
Page: 146

41. Socrates:
A. thought the state had obligations to the citizen
B. thought the citizen had obligations to the state
C. started the sophist philosophical tradition in Athens
D. was taught by Aristotle

Ans: B
Diff: M
Page: 149

42. After the Persian wars, Athens:
A. dropped out of the Spartan League
B. assumed a subordinate role within the Delian League
C. lost a war with Sparta
D. never managed to conquer the Melians

Ans: C
Diff: E
Page: 153

43. T F The Greek city-states were united both culturally and linguistically.

Ans: T
Diff: M
Page: 143

44. T F Greek city-states usually discouraged immigration from their territories.

Ans: F
Diff: H
Page: 145

45. T F Thucydides' work on the Peloponnesian war was more systematic and detailed than Herodotus' work on the Persian wars.

Ans: T
Diff: M
Page: 148

46. T F In Athens, the citizen had many rights, the state few.

Ans: F
Diff: H
Page: 150

47. Discuss the important reforms of Solon and Cleisthenes. Did these tend to make Athens more democratic or more autocratic?

Diff: M
Pages: 143-144

48. How did Socrates view the Athenian state, and what rights did he feel that state, and its citizens, were entitled to?

Diff: M
Page: 149

49. The archaeological discoveries of Heinrich Schliemann in the 1870s revealed evidence to support what had previously been considered myths concerning which two kingdoms?
A. Troy and Minos
B. Troy and Macedonia
C. Troy and Sparta
D. Troy and Mycenae

Ans: D
Diff: M
Page: 139

50. Which of the following events occurred first?
A. the 2nd Peloponnesian War
B. the Battle of Marathon
C. the burning of Persepolis
D. the construction of the Acropolis

Ans: B
Diff: M
Page: 140

51. Explain the significance of the poetry of Homer to our understanding of early Greece. What does he reveal about what was important to the early Greeks?

Diff: M
Page: 142

52. Explain Socrates' reasoning in passing up the chance to escape his sentence after being condemned to death on fabricated charges.

Diff: M
Page: 150

53. The greatest number of battles in the Persian wars occurred in which of the following locations?
A. Crete
B. Sicily
C. Anatolia
D. Attica

Ans: D
Diff: E
Page: 152

54. Compare the ideas of Socrates with those of Pericles concerning the concept of civic virtue.

Diff: H
Pages: 149-150, 153

55. Phillip II of Macedon:
A. conquered the Persian empire
B. was a skilled warrior, but a poor diplomat
C. wanted to bring peace to the Greek city-states
D. was tutored by Socrates

Ans: C
Diff: M
Page: 154

56. Alexander the Great:
A. forced conquered peoples to worship Greek gods and goddesses
B. typically ruled through local hierarchies
C. saw his empire slowly disintegrate during the last years of his life
D. never managed to conquer Egypt

Ans: B
Diff: M
Page: 155

57. Which of the following explains why Alexander failed to carry his empire as far as the Ganges in India?
A. His troops mutinied
B. He died before he could reach India
C. The Persian forces overwhelmed his troops
D. He lacked the financial resources to accomplish the task

Ans: A
Diff: E
Page: 156

58. Which two leaders built kingdoms from the wreckage of Alexander's empire?
A. Peisistratus and Xerxes
B. Demosthenes and Pericles
C. Ptolemy and Seleucus
D. Philipp II and Thebes

Ans: C
Diff: M
Page: 156

59. Which of the following empires began as city-states?
A. Egyptian and Persian
B. Mesopotamian and Greek
C. Macedonian and Greek
D. Mesopotamian and Egyptian

Ans: B
Diff: M
Page: 159

60. T F An important goal of Philip II was to liberate the Greek city-states in Asia Minor from Persian control.

Ans: T
Diff: E
Page: 154

61. T F One legacy of Alexander the Great was a the wide dispersion of Greek culture far beyond the Aegean.

Ans: T
Diff: E
Page: 157

62. T F Alexander governed his empire by first eliminating all traces of the existing indigenous institutions, then imposing the institutions of Hellenistic culture on all he conquered.

Ans: F
Diff: E
Page: 158

63. Explain the factors that contributed to the downfall of the empire established by Alexander the Great.

Diff: M
Page: 156

64. Write a comprehensive essay examining the legacy of Alexander the Great.

Diff: M
Pages: 157-158

65. Alexander the Great extended his empire as far east as which of the following?
A. Arabia
B. Egypt
C. the Aral Sea
D. the Indus River

Ans: D
Diff: E
Page: 154

66. Does historian Peter Green see Alexander the Great as a hero or a villain? Explain how Green arrived at this conclusion.

Diff: H
Page: 157

1. The city of Rome was founded in approximately:
A. 753 B.C.E.
B. 509 B.C.E.
C. 405 B.C.E.
D. 241 B.C.E.

Ans: A
Diff: E
Page: 163

2. Rome became a republic in this year:
A. 753 B.C.E.
B. 509 B.C.E.
C. 405 B.C.E.
D. 241 B.C.E.

Ans: B
Diff: E
Page: 164

3. Rome:
A. believed in the domino theory
B. never could expel the Greeks from southern Italy
C. usually chose conquest of a state rather than an alliance with it
D. often granted some level of Roman citizenship to conquered peoples

Ans: D
Diff: M
Pages: 165, 170

4. Carthage:
A. lay nearly 800 miles away from Italy
B. lost all three Punic Wars
C. had little military success when Hannibal invaded Italy
D. was eventually defeated by Rome, but was given an honored place within the empire

Ans: B
Diff: M
Page: 166

5. Which of the following was conquered last by Rome?
A. Gaul
B. Spain
C. Greece
D. Carthage

Ans: A
Diff: E
Page: 167

6. The Roman patron-client relationship:
A. applied primarily to the business sector
B. defined a state of reciprocity between the weak and the strong
C. led to the end of the role of the paterfamilias
D. allowed for an approximate equality between people of different classes

Ans: B
Diff: M
Page: 172

7. The Struggle of the Orders was:
A. primarily a religious conflict
B. a conflict between plebeians and patricians
C. settled when the patricians suppressed the plebeians by force
D. ameliorated substantially by the expansion of imperial Rome

Ans: B
Diff: E
Page: 173

8. The Gracchi:
A. managed to avoid violence
B. sought to shift the balance of power toward the upper classes
C. succeeded in achieving some of their desired reforms
D. severely damaged the stability of Rome

Ans: C
Diff: M
Page: 175

9. The triumvirate formed in 60 B.C.E. did NOT include this man:
A. Julius Caesar
B. Tiberius
C. Pompey
D. Crassus

Ans: B
Diff: M
Page: 178

10. Rome's military leaders:
A. were initially free from supervision by the senate
B. were initially free from supervision by the assembly
C. were initially constrained by elected civilian government
D. rarely became political leaders

Ans: C
Diff: H
Page: 178

11. Rome's armies:
A. spent little time developing new technology
B. were paid for primarily by taxes on Roman citizens
C. required few male citizens to actually serve in it
D. were often made up in part by men from conquered regions

Ans: D
Diff: M
Page: 182

12. During the height of the Roman Empire:
A. the most important import for Rome was wine
B. all major cities were relatively self-sufficient
C. Rome paid for most luxury goods with precious metals
D. It was not possible to obtain goods from India or China

Ans: C
Diff: M
Page: 184

13. Rome borrowed most from this culture:
A. Persian
B. Egyptian
C. Celtic
D. Greek

Ans: D
Diff: E
Page: 188

14. Stoicism held all of the following principles, except:
A. the world is an irrational place
B. a person should accept the world as it is
C. a person should accept all events dispassionately
D. a person should treat other people decently, even if they are from a lower social class

Ans: A
Diff: M
Page: 188

15. The belief system of Rome:
A. centered on the emperor as a god
B. prohibited paganism
C. did not allow any holidays
D. incorporated Christianity within a few decades of the death of Jesus

Ans: A
Diff: M
Page: 189

16. T F Romans thought of the Mediterranean Sea as being at the middle of their world.

Ans: T
Diff: E
Page: 163

17 T F Pompey conquered Gaul and brought it into the Roman Empire.

Ans: F
Diff: E
Page: 168

18. T F Plebians were the land holders who possessed longstanding hereditary connections to the state.

Ans: F
Diff: E
Page: 173

19. T F Intermarriage between the patricians and plebians was prohibited.

Ans: T
Diff: E
Page: 173

20. T F "Bread and circuses" exacerbated class conflict in Rome.

Ans: F
Diff: H
Page: 175

21. T F Julius Caesar ruled as dictator from 47 – 44 B.C.E.

Ans: T
Diff: E
Page: 179

22. T F England became part of the Roman empire in the 40s C.E.

Ans: T
Diff: E
Page: 181

23. T F When the Pax Romana faltered, trade declined.

Ans: T
Diff: M
Page: 187

24. T F Rome tolerated other religious sects as long as they did NOT challenge the authority of the empire or the emperor.

Ans: T
Diff: M
Page: 190

25. T F Christianity and Stoic philosophy had no significant common ground.

Ans: F
Diff: H
Page: 191

26. Describe the geographic extent of the Roman empire when it was at its height.

Diff: E
Pages: 165-168

27. Why were Rome and Carthage on a "collision course" in the Mediterranean region? What happened in the three Punic Wars and what was their ultimate outcome?

Diff: M
Pages: 165-167

28. Describe the nature of gender relationships in Rome. Did these change over time, and were such changes always favorable to women?

Diff: M
Page: 172

29. Discuss the nature of patron-client relations in Rome as they applied to the interactions of different classes, and then examine the Struggle of the Orders and the "bread and circuses" as examples of class conflict.

Diff: M
Pages: 171-173

30. Briefly present the reforms of the Gracchus brothers. Did they have any lasting effect?

Diff: M
Page: 174

31. Which of the following occurred first?
A. Sulla conquered Greece
B. the Third Punic War
C. Hannibal invaded Italy
D. Egypt was annexed

Ans: C
Diff: E
Page: 166

32. T F Roman women did not gain new rights until after citizenship was granted for all Roman males.

Ans: F
Diff: M
Page: 167

33. Which of the following was the first to be made part of the Roman empire?
A. Egypt
B. Britain
C. Syria
D. Sicily

Ans: D
Diff: M
Page: 168

34. Explain how Pompeii and Herculaneum have given historians good information about Roman life.

Diff: M
Page: 169

35. Describe the critiques of imperial Rome offered by historians Livy, Tacitus, and Dio Cassius. Which was most critical of the empire?

Diff: M
Page: 171

36. What did Augustus Caesar reveal about himself to the people of Rome in the *Res Gestae Divi Aususti*?

Diff: M
Page: 180

37. Explain the shortcoming of Rome's legal system identified by Juvenal.

Diff: M
Page: 182

38. The Silk Road linked which of the following cities?
A. Sarapion and Asabon
B. Luoyang and Bactra
C. Luoyang and Guangzhou
D. Antioch and Alexandria

Ans: B
Diff: E
Page: 183

39. Which of the following was the first emperor of the Flavian dynasty?
A. Flavian
B. Trajan
C. Valerian
D. Vespasian

Ans: D
Diff: E
Page: 184

40. Which of the following Greek and Roman Gods are linked correctly?
A. Zeus and Apollo
B. Aphrodite and Persephone
C. Dionysus and Bacchus
D. Ares and Mercury

Ans: C
Diff: E
Page: 189

41. The "barbarians":
A. were usually considered inferior by Romans
B. had their own written languages
C. were labeled by that term by the Romans because of their viciousness
D. built large cities beyond the boundaries of the Roman Empire

Ans: A
Diff: M
Page: 191

42. Once the Goths began to work with iron, contact with Greeks and Romans resulted in:
A. a Gothic victory against the Roman invaders
B. a dramatic increase in intertribal violence
C. the Germanic invasion of Britain
D. the development of more sophisticated tools and weapons

Ans: D
Diff: M
Page: 193

43. The fall of the Roman Empire:
A. occurred despite solid leadership over the final 200 years
B. was hastened by the actions of Germanic peoples
C. did not occur, according to most historians, until the Byzantine Empire was destroyed in 1453
D. was due primarily to the disrupting influence of Christianity

Ans: B
Diff: E
Page: 194

44. A key factor in the decline of Rome was:
A. a plague that killed nearly one quarter of the population in some areas
B. the superiority of Gothic weapons
C. the defeat of Augustus at the hand of the Han dynasty
D. the Visigoth invasion of Britain

Ans: A
Diff: E
Page: 194

45. Zenobia, widow of the leader of Palmyra:
A. led a revolt against the Roman Emperor Valerian
B. was defeated by the Mesopotamians in 273 C.E.
C. was defeated by the Egyptians in 273 C.E.
D. led a revolt against the Roman Emperor Aurelian

Ans: D
Diff: E
Page: 195

46. Attila, leader of the Huns:
A. invaded Italy in 451 C.E.
B. became the first barbarian king of Italy in 476 C.E.
C. executed Pope Leo I after he invaded Italy
D. deposed the last Roman emperor in the west

Ans: A
Diff: M
Page: 196

47. Christianity was initially embraced by the poor of the Roman Empire as a means of:
A. escaping the hopelessness of their situation
B. distinguishing themselves from the invading Germanic peoples
C. expressing their disaffection from the power of the Caesars
D. expressing their loyalty to the Holy Roman Empire

Ans: C
Diff: M
Page: 197

48. Under the leadership of Emperor Constantine:
A. the Roman Empire was purged of its eastern characteristics
B. Constantinople served as the sister-capital of Rome
C. the Justinian legal code was spread throughout the empire
D. the Hagia Sophia was constructed in 532 C.E.

Ans: B
Diff: E
Pages: 198, 201

49. The Byzantine Empire was centered in
A. Rome
B. Constantinople
C. Antioch
D. Cyrene

Ans: B
Diff: E
Page: 199

50. A significant reason that the Byzantine Empire survived for 1000 years after Rome had fallen was:
A. its legal separation of the socio-economic classes
B. the more extensive geographic scope of the eastern empire
C. its much more efficient administration of government
D. the lack of large urban centers

Ans: C
Diff: M
Page: 200

51. T F The Celts sacked Rome in 390 B.C.E.

Ans: T
Diff: E
Page: 192

52. T F The Saxons fled to Britain to escape the Germanic invasion.

Ans: F
Diff: E
Page: 193

53. T F Under the guidance of Diocletian, the Roman Empire became much less ostentatious

Ans: F
Diff: E
Page: 195

54. T F According to historian Edward Gibbon, Christianity turned people against secular power

Ans: T
Diff: M
Page: 197

55. T F The Monophysites did NOT believe that Jesus' nature was human

Ans: T
Diff: E
Page: 198

56. T F Emperor Justinian oversaw the codification of Roman law

Ans: T
Diff: E
Page: 198

57. T F The iconoclasts endeavored to restore religious icons to eastern churches

Ans: F
Diff: E
Page: 199

58. Describe the significant causes led to the decline of the Roman Empire

Diff: M
Pages: 196-197

59. What role did Christianity play in the downfall of the Roman Empire?

Diff: M
Page: 197

60. In an essay explain the decline and fall of the Roman Empire, and then, for contrast, explain why the Byzantine Empire managed to last another thousand years after the demise of its western sibling. End with informed speculation as to what the Roman Empire could have done to prolong its existence.

Diff: H
Pages: 198-200

61. Describe the impact of Islam on the Roman Empire

Diff: M
Pages: 198-199

62. Even after its fall, Rome continued to have an influence within the territories it once ruled. Write an essay that discusses the legacy of the Roman Empire.

Diff: M
Page: 201

63. Which of the following groups migrated to Carthage, then across the Mediterranean Sea to Rome?
A. Huns
B. Visigoths
C. Angles, Saxons, Jutes
D. Vandals, Alans, Sueves

Ans: D
Diff: E
Page: 192

64. T F The Huns left a rich store of archaeological remains.

Ans: F
Diff: E
Page: 194

65. Which of the following controlled the largest geographic region?
A. Kingdom of the Visigoths
B. Byzantine Empire
C. Kingdom of the Ostrogoths
D. Kingdom of the Vandals

Ans: B
Diff: E
Page: 195

66. T F After 566 C.E., the Byzantine Empire included Italy and Libya.

Ans: F
Diff: M
Page: 197

1. The Zhou dynasty:
A. created the first true Chinese empire
B. stayed strong up to the point it was overthrown
C. disintegrated, leading to the Warring States period
D. was briefly interrupted by a 24-year interregnum

Ans: C
Diff: M
Page: 205

2. The Warring States period:
A. was ended by the Zhou dynasty
B. led to the rule of the Qin dynasty
C. occurred in part in the first century B.C.E.
D. influenced the teachings of Laozi

Ans: B
Diff: M
Page: 205

3. Which dynasty completed the construction of the 1500-mile Great Wall of China?
A. Zhou
B. Han
C. Qin
D. Tang

Ans: C
Diff: E
Page: 206

4. Confucius:
A. was made a high ranking advisor to a Chinese leader
B. lived during the period of the Warring States
C. had little lasting impact on the conduct of government in China
D. felt that some people were born evil and could not be changed

Ans: B
Diff: M
Page: 208

5. Of the following, which was NOT one of the five texts canonized by Confucius?
A. *The Good Life*
B. *Book of Changes*
C. *Book of Songs*
D. *Rites and Rituals*

Ans: A
Diff: H
Page: 209

6. Qin dynasty administration was characterized by:
A. a faithfulness to feudalism
B. formalized, written rules
C. the appointment of officials based on family ties
D. adherence to the teachings of Laozi

Ans: B
Diff: M
Page: 211

7. Which ideology had the most influence on the Qin dynasty?
A. legalism
B. Daoism
C. Confucianism
D. paganism

Ans: A
Diff: M
Page: 211

8. Daoism:
A. is quite similar to Confucianism
B. stresses a closeness to the natural world
C. was developed primarily to guide statesmen
D. presents a detailed set of formal rules to guide society

Ans: B
Diff: M
Page: 212

9. The Mandate of Heaven:
A. was a personal god worshipped by emperors
B. blessed moral rulers
C. showed it was pleased by creating natural disasters
D. could allow a dynasty to rule forever

Ans: B
Diff: M
Page: 214

10. The fall of the Qin dynasty was hastened most by:
A. the hostility of the peasantry
B. a series of national disasters
C. astrologers predicting that the dynasty no longer had the mandate of heaven
D. Mongol invasions from the north

Ans: A
Diff: M
Page: 214

11. T F The Qin dynasty created the first Chinese Empire.

Ans: T
Diff: E
Page: 205

12. T F Laozi believed that stable government required strict laws strictly enforced.

Ans: F
Diff: M
Page: 212

13. T F Confucianism became an important philosophy of the Han empire.

Ans: T
Diff: M
Page: 209

14. T F Confucianism thought political leadership should be morally based

Ans: T
Diff: M
Page: 209

15. T F The fall of the Qin dynasty was hastened by political infighting.

Ans: T
Diff: E
Page: 214

16. The Qin dynasty created the first Chinese empire. Describe how it managed to create this empire, and also discuss how it sought to help the economy, the characteristics of the government administration it created, and why it fell from power.

Diff: H
Pages: 205-207

17. Describe the main tenets of Daoism.

Diff: M
Page: 212

18. T F The Chinese developed cannons before the Europeans.

Ans: T
Diff: E
Page: 207

19. T F Daoism developed before Confucianism.

Ans: T
Diff: E
Page: 208

20. First present the basic principles of Confucius' teachings. Then discuss the impact his teachings had during his lifetime and following his death.

Diff: M
Page: 210

21. T F The Han Empire extended far beyond that controlled by the Qin Dynasty.

Ans: T
Diff: E
Page: 213

22. Over the course of the Han dynasty, this group rose to the top of the social and political hierarchy:
A. scholars
B. merchants
C. priests
D. generals

Ans: A
Diff: M
Page: 215

23. Regarding military policy of the Han empire, it is true that:
A. nearly all able-bodied men had to serve in the military
B. the Han emperors were much less militaristic than the Qin emperors
C. there was little trouble with the tribes beyond the Great Wall
D. the Han military was at a disadvantage at times because it had no horses for a cavalry

Ans: A
Diff: M
Page: 217

24. Between the first recorded census of 2 C.E. and the second extant census of 140 C.E., the population of China:
A. sharply increased to 26 million people
B. sharply declined to only 10 million people
C. dropped sharply to 48 million people
D. increased dramatically to 22 million

Ans: C
Diff: M
Page: 218

25. Chinese silk reached Rome via the first silk route in:
A. 138 B.C.E.
B. 40 C.E.
C. 57 B.C.E.
D. 11 C.E.

Ans: C
Diff: E
Page: 219

26. Regarding economic policy of the Han empire, it is true that:
A. the empire had to make do with what it had when it was founded, since no new sources of wealth were discovered
B. Han emperors refused to nationalize private enterprise
C. Emperor Wu cut taxes
D. Confucians opposed military expansion in part because it was so costly

Ans: D
Diff: H
Page: 220

27. T F Both men and women could become Confucian scholars.

Ans: T
Diff: E
Page: 216

28. T F In the Han dynasty, women were expected to say what they thought and be independent.

Ans: F
Diff: E
Page: 216

29. T F Chinese silk did NOT reach Europe until after the fall of the Han dynasty.

Ans: F
Diff: H
Page: 219

30. Confucianism had five significant influences on the Han dynasty. Describe them.

Diff: M
Page: 215

31. Describe the events that brought about the end of the Han dynasty.

Diff: M
Page: 221

32. What advice did Ban Zhao offer to women in Han Society?

Diff: M
Page: 216

33. Sima Qian:
A. was always treated with respect by the ruler of China
B. began the tradition of writing down Chinese history
C. stuck to the study of people and events
D. wrote a nearly complete history of China

Ans: D
Diff: M
Page: 217

34. Describe the events that occurred during the first two centuries C.E. that resulted in a major redistribution of the Chinese population.

Diff: M
Page: 218

35. The "three kingdoms and six dynasties" period:
A. began after the fall of the Tang dynasty
B. managed to maintain the dominant culture and ethics of earlier times
C. was a dismal time for the practice of Chinese arts
D. saw many Chinese near border areas drop the Chinese language in favor of barbarian tongues

Ans: B
Diff: M
Page: 222

36. Buddhism in China:
A. had little lasting impact
B. came by way of Japan
C. eventually gained millions of followers
D. had little in common with either Confucianism or Daoism

Ans: C
Diff: M
Page: 224

37. The Sui dynasty:
A. came between the Qin and Han dynasties
B. was founded by a Confucius scholar
C. initially had the loyalty of peasant farmers
D. decentralized authority, giving more independent power to local levels of government

Ans: C
Diff: M
Page: 224

38. The Grand Canal, completed during the Sui dynasty linked which of the following?
A. the Yangzi and the Yellow River systems
B. the Yangzi and the Huang He
C. the Yangzi and the Mekong
D. the Yangzi and the Ganges

Ans: A
Diff: E
Page: 224

39. The Tang dynasty:
A. presided during a major flowering of Chinese poetry
B. made major changes in the policies of the previous dynasty
C. abandoned the imperial examination system
D. persecuted Buddhism

Ans: A
Diff: M
Page: 226

40. T F After the fall of the Han dynasty, China was divided into three states.

Ans: T
Diff: E
Page: 222

41. T F Buddhism had a divisive effect on China

Ans: F
Diff: M
Page: 224

42. T F The Sui dynasty restored the economic productivity of China

Ans: T
Diff: E
Page: 224

43. T F The Tany dynasty rejected the policies of the Sui.

Ans: F
Diff: M
Page: 225

44. What happened to Chinese culture, ethics, and arts during the "three kingdoms and six dynasties" period?

Diff: M
Page: 222

45. Compare, contrast, and analyze the military, political, and economic policies of the Sui and Tang dynasties.

Diff: H
Pages: 224-225

46. Describe the impact of the Guangdong, Tongli, Shanyang, Yongli, and Jiangnan canal systems on Chinese commerce.

Diff: M
Page: 222

47. T F In 751 C.E. the Tang Empire reached its western limits at the Talas River.

Ans: T
Diff: E
Page: 226

48. Describe the ways in which Du Fu's *Ballad of the Army Carts* reflects Confucianism.

Diff: H
Page: 229

49. Vietnam:
A. has been independent of China for most of the last 2000 years
B. rejected Confucianist teachings
C. was more influenced by Korea than China
D. had a love/hate relationship with China

Ans: D
Diff: M
Page: 231

50. Korea broke free from direct Chinese control:
A. following the collapse of the Zhou dynasty in 256 B.C.E.
B. following the collapse of the Han dynasty in 220 C.E.
C. following the collapse of the Qin dynasty in 206 B.C.E.
D. following the collapse of the Shi dynasty in 618 C.E.

Ans: B
Diff: E
Page: 231

51. Japan:
A. was conquered twice by China
B. was careful to keep its borders closed to immigrants during its early years
C. modeled its art on that of the southeast Asian islands
D. accepted the cultural hegemony of China

Ans: D
Diff: M
Page: 232

52. The seventeen-point program adopted by Japan:
A. was adopted around the year 1410
B. included reverence for Buddhism
C. was designed to exclude any Chinese influence
D. did not provide for the collection of taxes

Ans: B
Diff: H
Page: 233

53. China and Rome were similar in all of the following ways, except for:
A. the role of the emperor
B. religious policies
C. concentration of wealth
D. influence on neighbors

Ans: D
Diff: M
Page: 235

54. China and Rome were different in all of the following ways, except for:
A. gender relationships
B. language policy
C. longevity
D. geopolitical characteristics

Ans: A
Diff: M
Page: 236

55. T F The Chinese Empire existed for nearly 1400 years without any break-ups of its territory into smaller units.

Ans: F
Diff: M
Page: 229

56. T F The Chinese had a major influence on Korea.

Ans: T
Diff: E
Page: 231

57. T F Neither the Roman Empire nor the Chinese Empire put much effort into public works projects.

Ans: F
Diff: M
Page: 236

58. In what ways did China influence the social, political, and religious characteristics of Japan?

Diff: M
Pages: 232-233

59. Write an essay that describes four important differences and five important similarities between China and Rome.

Diff: M
Pages: 234-237

60. In which of the following are the dynasties arranged in proper chronological order?
A. Shang, Sui, Tang, Han
B. Qin, Han, Tang, Sui
C. Shang, Zhou, Han, Qin
D. Qin, Han, Sui, Tang

Ans: D
Diff: M
Page: 230

61. T F In Chang'an, the imperial palace is located in the center of the walled city.

Ans: F
Diff: E
Page: 232

1. The Indian subcontinent includes all of the following areas, except:
A. Tibet
B. Bhutan
C. Bangladesh
D. Nepal

Ans: A
Diff: E
Page: 241

2. Since 3000 B.C.E., most invasions of India have come from the:
A. ocean
B. southeast
C. northwest
D. southwest

Ans: C
Diff: H
Page: 241

3. Of the following, who came closest to unifying the entire Indian subcontinent?
A. Chandragupta Maurya
B. Asoka
C. Kanishka
D. Alexander the Great

Ans: B
Diff: M
Page: 241

4. Aryan immigrants to the Indus valley:
A. came from Europe
B. came from central Asia
C. came from the Iranian plateau
D. were called Aryan because the language they spoke belonged to the Indo-Aryan language group

Ans: D
Diff: M
Page: 242

5. Of the following, which primarily presents legends and folk tales?
A. the Vedas
B. the *Mahabharata*
C. the Puranas
D. the *Ramayana*

Ans: C
Diff: H
Page: 242

6. Which of the following statements about the *Ramayana* is incorrect?
A. It leads some women to be critical of Rama's actions toward his wife Sita
B. It leads some men to applaud Sita's actions toward her husband
C. It is interpreted differently in different parts of the Hindu world
D. It refers to an earlier time than that depicted in the *Mahabharata*

Ans: D
Diff: M
Page: 244

7. The Aryan peoples in India:
A. first arrived in the Indus valley in 1000 B.C.E.
B. were expelled from the region by the Maurya dynasty
C. formed political groupings called *junapadas*
D. spoke a Semitic language

Ans: C
Diff: M
Page: 246

8. T F The Vedas are secular, historical accounts.

Ans: F
Diff: E
Page: 242

9. T F *Bhagavad-Gita* examines warfare, life, death, and rebirth.

Ans: T
Diff: M
Page: 243

10. T F The *Ramayana* and the *Mahabharata* both relate historical events of early Indian history.

Ans: F
Diff: M
Page: 243

11. T F The *Ramayana* is interpreted differently in different parts of the Hindu world.

Ans: T
Diff: M
Page: 244

12. T F The *Artha-sastra* includes codes of law and statecraft.

Ans: T
Diff: E
Page: 245

13. First present the basic stories of the *Mahabharata* and the *Ramayana*. Then describe why the *Mahabharata* is so important for understanding India's culture.

Diff: M
Pages: 243-244

14. Describe the perceptions of India expressed by foreign Buddhist pilgrims as they traveled to India.

Diff: M
Page: 245

15. Why has the Indus valley yielded more archaeological artifacts than the Ganges valley?

Diff: E
Page: 242

16. Which of the following was written first?
A. the *Bhagavad-Gita*
B. the Puranas
C. Sangam poetry
D. the *Mahabharata* and *Ramayana*

Ans: B
Diff: E
Page: 243

17. T F Hindu gained ascendancy over Buddhism during India's "golden age".

Ans: F
Diff: E
Page: 244

18. The *Artha-sastra*:
A. was written by a minister serving the Gupta Empire
B. has been known to historians since the early 1500s
C. held that "the enemy of my friend is my enemy"
D. used the analogy that big fish eat littler fish

Ans: D
Diff: H
Page: 248

19. The most important of the internal functions of the Mauryan empire was:
A. ensuring that citizens had the opportunity to pursue the four major goals of Hindu philosophy
B. enforcing gender roles
C. maintaining the caste system
D. regulating the activities of guilds

Ans: A
Diff: M
Page: 248

20. The caste system of India:
A. was constructed primarily to regulate gender relations
B. held that a person's socio-economic status was hereditary
C. forbade upward class mobility
D. consisted of four classes: rulers, priests, warriors, laborers

Ans: B
Diff: M
Page: 248

21. Asoka:
A. practiced peace during his entire rule
B. converted to Buddhism
C. left no written record
D. instituted policies damaging to merchants and guilds

Ans: B
Diff: E
Page: 250

22. The Kushana:
A. invaded India just prior to the rule of the Mauryan family
B. came from the Iranian plateau
C. left no artifacts traceable to the time of their rule
D. were supporters of Buddhism

Ans: D
Diff: M
Page: 251

23. The Gupta Empire asserted the most control over:
A. conquered territories
B. local government
C. the heartland of the empire
D. regional government

Ans: C
Diff: H
Page: 252

24. The Guptas:
A. encouraged a resurgence of Hindu philosophy
B. discouraged the arts, since they felt they stirred up anti-government feelings
C. discouraged the use of Sanskrit and encouraged the use of Urdu
D. shut down most Buddhist monasteries and centers of learning

Ans: A
Diff: M
Page: 252

25. T F Asoka's son, a Buddhist missionary, succeeded in converting Sri Lanka to Buddhism.

Ans: T
Diff: E
Page: 250

26. T F The Gupta Empire followed immediately after the Maurya Empire.

Ans: F
Diff: E
Page: 251

27. T F The rule of the Gupta Empire has been called India's golden age.

Ans: T
Diff: E
Page: 252

28. During the time of the Gupta Empire, Buddhism gained almost complete ascendancy over Hinduism.

Ans: F
Diff: M
Page: 253

29. The rule of the Gupta Empire has been referred to as indirect rule. Why is this an apt description, especially in light of the way most empires ruled their domains?

Diff: M
Page: 252

30. The time of the Gupta Empire has been called India's golden age. Why?

Diff: M
Pages: 252-253

31. T F Asoka extended the Mauryan Empire south into the Deccan.

Ans: T
Diff: E
Page: 247

32. Describe and evaluate the rule of Asoka, including his foreign conquests, the results of his conversion to Buddhism, and the nature of his administration.

Diff: H
Page: 249

33. T F The Gupta Empire spanned the subcontinent from the Ganges to the Indus.

Ans: T
Diff: E
Page: 252

34. Huna control of India was effectively ended when the Turkic and Persian armies defeated the Hunas in
A. Kashmir
B. Bactria
C. Lanka
D. Deccan

Ans: B
Diff: E
Page: 254

35. Which of the following is NOT a legacy of the Hunas?
A. dismemberment of the Gupta empire
B. introduction of new groups into areas already settled
C. increase in inter-regional trade
D. flowering of Hindu philosophy

Ans: C
Diff: H
Page: 255

36. India's "adivasis":
A. are well described in ancient historical records
B. usually live in the less-accessible areas
C. farm some of India's richest soil
D. have rarely been able to assert any independence

Ans: B
Diff: M
Page: 256

37. Funan:
A. did not allow the influence of Buddhism into its territory
B. built Angkor Wat
C. encouraged Hinduism
D. controlled only a small area around the mouth of the Mekong River

Ans: C
Diff: E
Page: 258

38. Angkor Wat:
A. is situated in the southern tip of India
B. is dedicated to Vishnu, one of the major Hindu gods
C. was once the center of the Maurya dynasty
D. was built around 200 C.E.

Ans: B
Diff: M
Page: 259

39. T F The major regions of India often have their own languages.

Ans: T
Diff: E
Page: 255

40. T F Inhabitants of India apparently did little if any travel by ocean for the purpose of trade.

Ans: F
Diff: M
Page: 257

41. T F The independent Funan state established hegemony over southern Vietnam and Cambodia

Ans: T
Diff: E
Page: 258

42. What were the major impacts of the Huna invasions on India? How was power distributed throughout the subcontinent for the thousand or so years after the invasions?

Diff: M
Pages: 254-255

43. Describe the religion and geographical extent of the Funan kingdom.

Diff: M
Page: 258

44. T F For almost a thousand years, India was ruled by many powerful ethnic kingdoms, rather than by a centralized empire.

Ans: T
Diff: E
Page: 255

45. T F Sangam poetry examined the interplay of love and warfare.

Ans: T
Diff: E
Page: 256

46. Findings at Roman trade sites dating to about zero C.E. suggest that of the following groups, this group was least involved in ocean trade between the Roman Empire and India:
A. Arabs
B. Indians
C. Jews
D. Romans

Ans: B
Diff: M
Page: 257

47. Which empire or series of empires left the least amount of detailed records?
A. Indian empires
B. Roman Empire
C. Chinese empires
D. Ottoman Empire

Ans: A
Diff: M
Page: 260

48. Asoka's empire:
A. included the island of Sri Lanka
B. was overthrown by barbarian invasions from the north
C. was not described in known historical records until a find about 100 years ago
D. expelled many Hindus

Ans: C
Diff: H
Page: 260

49. Over the last 2000 years, India:
A. has managed to maintain administrative continuity
B. has been ruled by one empire after another
C. hosted empires that never managed to expand beyond the subcontinent
D. has become primarily a Muslim state

Ans: C
Diff: E
Page: 260

50. In India's history over the last 2400 years, this type of attachment has been the most transient:
A. political
B. religious
C. familial
D. caste

Ans: A
Diff: H
Pages: 260-261

51. The political experience shared by India, Rome and China was:
A. the rejection of Buddhism
B. the development of a long-standing, geographically expansive empire
C. widespread internal revolts
D. invasion and at least partial conquest by the Hunas and by the peoples they displaced

Ans: D
Diff: M
Page: 260

52. T F The rock and pillar inscriptions of Asoka were deciphered in the early eighteenth century.

Ans: F
Diff: E
Page: 260

53. T F Asoka embraced the excessive use of force throughout his reign.

Ans: F
Diff: E
Page: 260

54. T F Overall, the state in India presided over pre-existing social institutions.

Ans: T
Diff: E
Page: 261

55. Explain the relationship between the state and Indian social institutions.

Diff: M
Page: 261

56. Write an essay comparing the India of 300 B.C.E. to 1500 C.E. with the Chinese and Roman empires in the following areas: continuity of bureaucracy, succession of leadership, ability to keep the core empire together.

Diff: H
Pages: 260-261

1. According to historian Mircea Eliade, the "sacred":
A. must be experienced internally
B. cannot provide a deeper sense of significance to life
C. was not understood by "primitive" man
D. is distinct from mundane acts such as eating or sexual activity

Ans: A
Diff: E
Page: 268

2. Evidence that Neanderthals expressed religious beliefs includes:
A. carved ivory statues in gravesites
B. glass beads in gravesites
C. flint tools and prepared food in gravesites
D. all of the above

Ans: C
Diff: M
Page: 268

3. T F Stonehenge was a temple of the Druids.

Ans: F
Diff: E
Page: 269

4. T F The caste system of Hinduism provided India with a sense of unity.

Ans: T
Diff: E
Page: 269

5. Explain the how burial rituals demonstrate the human desire for a relationship with the sacred.

Diff: M
Page: 268

6. According to Martin Luther, one of the most significant problems of the mid-fifteenth century Church was:
A. its inability to raise the funds necessary to support missionary activities
B. its refusal to sell "indulgences"
C. the granting of forgiveness of sin in exchange for donations
D. its refusal to look after its financial situation

Ans: C
Diff: M
Page: 385

7. Which of the following religions advocates a complete separation of spiritual and commercial matters?
A. Islam
B. Christianity
C. Hinduism
D. Judaism

Ans: B
Diff: E
Pages: 386-387

8. T F One category of the Hindu caste system is composed of business people.

Ans: T
Diff: E
Page: 387

9. T F Islam and Hinduism integrate business practices with religious rituals.

Ans: T
Diff: M
Pages: 386-387

10. Explain the relationship between religion and business. Are they mutually exclusive?

Diff: M
Pages: 385-387

1. The oldest religion still in practice is:
A. Buddhism
B. Judaism
C. Hinduism
D. Christianity

Ans: C
Diff: E
Page: 271

2. The *Rigveda*:
A. consists primarily of prayers and chants
B. is the youngest of the major writings of Hinduism
C. presents Hinduism as a monotheistic religion
D. offers no definitive answers to the question of how the world was created

Ans: D
Diff: M
Page: 275

3. The caste system in India:
A. officially provides for six castes
B. is officially sanctioned by the *Rigveda*
C. does not provide for a soldier class
D. has no relevance in the India of today

Ans: B
Diff: M
Page: 275

4. Lord Krishna:
A. was always either a king, brahmin, or general whenever he appeared to humans
B. was the main character in the *Ramayana*
C. is the creator of the universe
D. is usually depicted with blue or black skin

Ans: D
Diff: M
Pages: 274, 276

5. Which of the following statements drawn from the teachings of the Upanishads is NOT correct?
A. *Dharma* is a set of proper duties that can vary from individual to individual
B. An *atman* that does not reach *moksha* will continue in *samsara*
C. In the last stage of life one should be a *brahmacharya*
D. *Karma* can be either bad or good

Ans: C
Diff: H
Page: 279

6. According to the Upanishads, the time for "forest wandering," or reflection, is the:
A. first stage of life
B. second stage of life
C. third stage of life
D. fourth stage of life

Ans: C
Diff: M
Page: 279

7. The Puranas focus least on this:
A. the deep philosophical concepts of Hinduism
B. stories of goddesses
C. stories of gods
D. folk tales

Ans: A
Diff: M
Page: 282

8. Regarding Hinduism, it is most true that:
A. temples were usually directed by the peasants
B. *brahmin* priests often supported local rulers
C. *brahmin* priests often donated their land to the king
D. religion and politics were strictly separated

Ans: B
Diff: M
Page: 283

9. Outside the Indian subcontinent, Hinduism historically gained the most new converts in:
A. Arabia
B. China
C. Southeast Asia
D. the Horn of Africa

Ans: C
Diff: E
Page: 284

10. T F Hinduism absorbed the gods of many local tribes.

Ans: T
Diff: M
Page: 274

11. T F The *Ramayana* includes the *Bhagavadgita*.

Ans: F
Diff: M
Page: 279

12. T F Ritualistic sex is an integral part of Bhakti Hinduism.

Ans: F
Diff: E
Page: 281

13. Present and give a one- to two-sentence description of the characteristics found in most religions.

Diff: M
Page: 272

14. Give a five- to six-sentence description of what is known about the historical origins of Hinduism.

Diff: M
Page: 273

15. Describe the following concepts of Hinduism: *atman, samsara, dharma, karma, moksha, maya*, the four stages of the life cycle.

Diff: M
Page: 279

16. What is the main focus of Bhakti and how does it relate to traditional Hinduism?

Diff: E
Page: 281

17. T F The Puranas were written before the *Rigveda*.

Ans: F
Diff: E
Page: 273

18. T F Hinduism is strongly connected to the sacred geography of the Indian subcontinent.

Ans: T
Diff: E
Page: 274

19. The Hindu culture developed before which of the following religious cultures?
A. Jewish
B. Islamic
C. Hittite
D. Sumerian

Ans: B
Diff: M
Page: 275

20. Currently, the religion with the second-highest number of adherents in the world is:
A. Islam
B. Christianity
C. Hinduism
D. Buddhism

Ans: A
Diff: M
Page: 277

21. The dance of this god symbolizes the cycle of creation and destruction:
A. Shiva
B. Krishna
C. Brahma
D. Vishnu

Ans: A
Diff: M
Page: 278

22. T F Krishna is an incarnation of Vishnu.

Ans: T
Diff: E
Page: 278

23. T F The Vedas encompass the "divine knowledge" of Hinduism.

Ans: T
Diff: E
Page: 279

24. In the *Bhagavadgita*:
A. Arjuna learns that pacifism is the proper way of the Hindu
B. Krishna is the commander of Arjuna
C. Krishna tells Arjuna that Arjuna is not truly a warrior
D. Arjuna learns that he should follow his *dharma*, whether he wants to or not

Ans: D
Diff: M
Page: 281

25. T F Trade routes connected Gupta India directly to Africa.

Ans: T
Diff: M
Page: 284

26. Of the theories that explain the spread of Hinduism, which do you find most convincing? Explain.

Diff: M
Page: 286

27. Buddhism:
A. began in Tibet
B. did not have a specific founder
C. had an order of monks
D. did not develop scripture

Ans: C
Diff: E
Page: 286

28. Through the course of history, Hinduism won out over Buddhism in this region:
A. India
B. Tibet
C. Sri Lanka
D. Korea

Ans: A
Diff: E
Page: 286

29. The Buddha was:
A. born in southern India
B. a member of the *brahmin* caste
C. forecast to be either a businessman or a farmer
D. a wandering ascetic for several years

Ans: D
Diff: M
Page: 286

30. While sitting under a tree at Bodh Gaya, the Buddha:
A. attained enlightenment
B. rededicated himself to asceticism
C. developed the four-fold path
D. remained in meditation for 100 days and nights

Ans: A
Diff: M
Page: 286

31. For the Buddha, the source of unhappiness in the world was:
A. desire
B. the wish to reach enlightenment
C. the inability of many souls to get incarnated into healthy bodies
D. the inaccurate teachings of the Hindu *brahmins*

Ans: A
Diff: E
Page: 286

32. Members of this group were least likely to convert to Buddhism from Hinduism:
A. priest caste
B. warrior caste
C. businessman caste
D. lower castes

Ans: A
Diff: M
Page: 287

33. The Buddha taught all of the following, except:
A. the existence of the soul
B. the non-existence of god
C. the way to reach nirvana
D. the possibility of leaving the cycle of birth and rebirth

Ans: A
Diff: H
Page: 287

34. The Sangha:
A. was only open to certain castes
B. freely admitted women
C. required a vow of obedience
D. advocated celibacy for monks

Ans: D
Diff: M
Page: 288

35. Mahayana Buddhism:
A. took its name from the Sanskrit term for "lesser vehicle"
B. never presented a serious challenge to Theravada Buddhism
C. believed in the bodhisattva concept
D. argued there was no heaven

Ans: C
Diff: E
Page: 289

36. Buddhism in China:
A. enjoyed immediate and lasting favor from the ruling classes
B. came from India via sea trading routes
C. conflicted sharply with Daoism
D. developed a sect called Chan, which later became Zen in Japan

Ans: D
Diff: M
Page: 295

37. Shinto beliefs:
A. found spirits inherent in nature
B. believe that only the one god can bring salvation
C. prohibit worship of the sun or any sun gods or goddesses
D. have had no relevance in Japan since the Meiji restoration in the nineteenth century

Ans: A
Diff: M
Page: 297

38. Shingon Buddhism:
A. prohibits music
B. prohibits dancing
C. believes in the recitation of mantras
D. holds that the most important phrase is "Praise to Amida Buddha"

Ans: C
Diff: M
Page: 300

39. Hinduism and Buddhism were similar in all of the following aspects, except:
A. the degree of respect they gave to *brahmins*
B. their development of sacred languages
C. their place of origin
D. their belief in reincarnation

Ans: A
Diff: M
Page: 301

40. T F Some Hindus consider Jainism a branch of Hinduism, but Jains disagree.

Ans: T
Diff: M
Page: 293

41. T F Jainism rejects the caste system and embraces nonviolence.

Ans: T
Diff: E
Page: 293

42. T F One of the key areas of difference between Buddhism and Confucianism was the attitude toward government control

Ans: T
Diff: M
Page: 294

43. T F Chan/Zen Buddhism stresses the importance of meditation.

Ans: T
Diff: M
Page: 295

44. T F The Buddhist clergy in Japan stayed out of politics.

Ans: F
Diff: M
Page: 299

45. T F Both Hinduism and Buddhism developed sacred languages.

Ans: T
Diff: E
Page: 301

46. Describe the life of the Buddha up to the time he reached enlightenment. Then describe the following Buddhist concepts: the four noble truths, the eightfold path, and the existence or non-existence of *atman* and Brahman.

Diff: H
Page: 286

47. What were the general rules of the Sangha?

Diff: M
Page: 287

48. Discuss and analyze various hypotheses on why Buddhism declined so drastically in India.

Diff: H
Page: 290

49. What are the most important aspects of Chan/Zen Buddhism, the Pure Land Sect of Buddhism, and Shingon Buddhism?

Diff: M
Pages: 295-296

50. List and describe the similarities between Hinduism and Buddhism.

Diff: M
Page: 301

51. Describe the relationship between the spread and development of Hinduism and Buddhism, and the rise and fall of political leaders.

Diff: M
Page: 302

52. How does Buddha define proper gender roles?

Diff: M
Page: 287

53. List Buddha's Four Noble Truths. Where does this path lead?

Diff: E
Page: 289

54. The Buddhist center furthest from the site of Buddha's enlightenment is located in:
A. Bamiyan
B. Kotabangun
C. Edo
D. Kandy

Ans: C
Diff: M
Page: 291

55. Based on the poem discovered in the Dunhuang cave, what was the role of women in the Tang dynasty? In what ways does this poem reflect Buddhist principles?

Diff: M
Page: 295

1. Judaism:
A. began when Adam made a pact with God that Adam's descendants would always worship God
B. is basically a polytheistic religion
C. once contained nearly one-fifth of the world population
D. has had a role in history that is disproportionate to the number of its followers

Ans: D
Diff: E
Page: 307

2. Which of the following is NOT one of the books that form the Torah?
A. Ezekiel
B. Leviticus
C. Numbers
D. Exodus

Ans: A
Diff: M
Page: 310

3. The Torah:
A. was written just before the birth of Christ
B. is notable for its absence of miracles
C. has changed little since it was written
D. begins with the exodus of the Jews from Egypt

Ans: C
Diff: M
Page: 310

4. Which of the following was NOT a principal belief that came from the early scriptures of Judaism?
A. God demands obedience
B. Several dispersed homelands for Jews
C. A legal code to shape behavior
D. Jews as a community blessed by God

Ans: B
Diff: M
Page: 311

5. The later books of Jewish scripture:
A. do not include either the Nevi'im or the Ketuvim
B. conclude with the four gospels of Jesus Christ
C. describe many historical events and people that have been independently verified
D. did not survive the diaspora

Ans: C
Diff: M
Page: 313

6. The return of the Jews to Canaan:
A. was accompanied by warfare
B. left them still searching for the promised land
C. was followed within a few years by the formation of a strong, unified state
D. occurred around 400 B.C.E.

Ans: A
Diff: H
Page: 313

7. The rule of Saul, David, and Solomon:
A. eventually led to the creation of the Judaea and Israel
B. was characterized by the separation of state and religion
C. is considered by most modern historians to have been weak and ineffectual
D. helped the Jews build up the strength necessary to conquer the promised land

Ans: A
Diff: M
Page: 314

8. According to Jewish beliefs, God:
A. has always maintained the same outlook toward the Jews
B. is accessible only through rabbis
C. would sometimes dialogue with humans
D. should be invoked by repeatedly chanting his name out loud

Ans: C
Diff: M
Page: 316

9. Regarding gender relations, the Hebrew scriptures:
A. hold that God has equal amounts of male and female qualities
B. give women fewer civil rights than men have
C. give women more religious rights than men have
D. advocate polygamy

Ans: B
Diff: E
Page: 317

10. Which diaspora caused the most fundamental and lasting change for Jews?
A. Babylonian diaspora
B. diaspora in Egypt
C. diaspora at the hands of the Assyrians
D. diaspora at the hands of the Romans

Ans: D
Diff: M
Page: 319

11. T F Abraham was the leader of the first unified Jewish state.

Ans: F
Diff: M
Page: 309

12. T F Moses received the Ten Commandments after leading the Jews to the promised land.

Ans: F
Diff: M
Page: 309

13. T F In the Torah, God changes as a moral force over time.

Ans: T
Diff: M
Page: 315

14. T F Nearly all Jews exiled to Babylon chose to return to Jewish lands after the exile was ended.

Ans: F
Diff: H
Page: 318

15. The Torah is a central document of Judaism. Briefly discuss the history covered by the Torah, and then describe the essential beliefs found in the Torah that guided and continue to guide the Jewish nation.

Diff: M
Pages: 309-311

16. As portrayed in the Torah, God changed over time. What characteristics did he have in the early Jewish period and how did these change?

Diff: M
Page: 315

17. After the Jewish state split into the separate kingdoms of Israel and Judaea, several prophets appeared with messages for the Jewish people. What spurred these prophets to action? What was the thrust of their teachings?

Diff: H
Page: 315

18. Briefly describe the consequences of Roman exile for the Jews.

Diff: E
Page: 319

19. Which of the following happened most recently?
A. Jews enslaved in Egypt
B. Moses leads the Jews
C. Jewish kingdom split into Judaea and Israel
D. Formulation of Jewish legal codes

Ans: C
Diff: E
Page: 308

20. Before the death of Solomon in 926 B.C.E., the Jewish state controlled the area from the Euphrates in the north to the southern border at:
A. the Dead Sea
B. the Sea of Galilee
C. the Mediterranean Sea
D. the Red Sea

Ans: D
Diff: E
Page: 310

21. T F According to the Torah, Moses received the Ten Commandments atop Mount Ebal

Ans: F
Diff: E
Page: 312

22. Which of the following festivals occurs in the Hebrew month, Nisan?
A. Shavuot
B. Hannukah
C. Pesach
D. Yom Kippur

Ans: C
Diff: E
Page: 317

23. T F After the Romans expelled the Jews from Judaea, Jewish communities were established throughout the Mediterranean.

Ans: T
Diff: E
Page: 320

24. Jesus Christ:
A. aimed his message at the middle class
B. was considered a threat by the Roman government
C. was crucified when he was about 50 years old
D. sought support from Jewish religious authorities

Ans: B
Diff: E
Page: 321

25. Jesus' most important commandment was to:
A. love your neighbor
B. love God
C. give to the poor
D. honor your father and mother

Ans: B
Diff: M
Page: 325

26. For Paul, the most important criterion for being a Christian was:
A. observance of Jewish ritual laws
B. being born into a Christian family
C. low socioeconomic status
D. faith

Ans: D
Diff: M
Page: 327

27. Paul:
A. felt that married clergy were closer to God than single clergy
B. opposed slavery in both principle and practice
C. was Jesus' most devoted disciple in the years prior to Jesus' death
D. sought to subordinate women in the church

Ans: D
Diff: H
Page: 328

28. In the year 250 C.E., most of Rome's Christians were members of the:
A. lower class
B. middle class
C. upper class
D. military

Ans: A
Diff: E
Page: 329

29. Emperor Constantine:
A. failed in his effort to convert his mother to Christianity
B. never managed to gain control of the western portions of the Roman empire
C. gave equal treatment to all religions practiced within his empire
D. had a vision that helped convert him to Christianity

Ans: D
Diff: M
Page: 329

30. Emperor Theodosius:
A. practiced religious tolerance
B. made Christianity the official religion of the Roman Empire
C. was overthrown by Constantine
D. gave special privileges to Jews

Ans: B
Diff: M
Page: 329

31. Augustine:
A. held that the spiritual cannot be separated from the political
B. was a bishop in Rome who eventually became the first pope
C. taught that the path to salvation was through human reason
D. supported the separation of church and state

Ans: D
Diff: H
Page: 331

32. The dogma of the early Christian Church:
A. was conducive to doctrinal disagreement
B. conclusively argued that God was more divine than Jesus
C. led to violent confrontation between competing factions
D. fostered equal rights for women

Ans: C
Diff: M
Page: 332

33. Which of the following Jewish groups stayed aloof from politics and preached that the end of the world was imminent?
A. Pharisees
B. Sadducees
C. Essenes
D. Zealots

Ans: C
Diff: M
Page: 321

34. T F Jesus held that economic status could have a strong impact on whether or not a person would get into heaven.

Ans: T
Diff: M
Page: 325

35. T F Paul thought it possible for humans to overcome original sin.

Ans: T
Diff: M
Page: 327

36. T F Persecution by the Romans led to a decline in Christian conversions.

Ans: F
Diff: M
Page: 329

37. T F Pelagius preached that humans could choose between good and evil and thus determine their own fate.

Ans: T
Diff: E
Page: 332

38. Describe the four major Jewish factions that existed at the time of Jesus. Which group do you think Jesus would have identified with most strongly? Which do you think he would have opposed the most strongly?

Diff: M
Page: 321

39. Paul became the most important organizer and proselytizer of the new Christian faith. He also developed many doctrines of Christianity. Write an essay that discusses his missionary activities; his views on gender relations, slavery, and criteria for membership in the church; and his teachings on Christian philosophy and ritual.

Diff: H
Pages: 326-328

40. Describe and analyze the concept of "original sin" and Paul's interpretation of it in light of Jesus' teachings and life.

Diff: M
Page: 327

41. At the time of Jesus, which of the following directly controlled the largest geographic territory?
A. Rome
B. Herod
C. Philip
D. Jesus

Ans: A
Diff: E
Page: 322

42. The four gospels were written:
A. between about 70 C.E. and 100 C.E.
B. by the apostle Paul
C. just after the crucifixion of Jesus
D. with the strict guidance of Roman censors

Ans: A
Diff: M
Page: 323

43. The Sermon on the Mount was one of the most important presentations of Jesus' thought. What were the main points of this sermon, and for what class of people were the words primarily intended?

Diff: M
Page: 324

44. Which of the following locations was NOT visited by Paul on his fourth journey, 59-62 C.E.?
A. Crete
B. Malta
C. Italy
D. Macedonia

Ans: D
Diff: E
Page: 326

45. Which Christian festival commemorates the beginning of the Apostles' preaching mission?
A. Feast of Annunciation
B. Pentecost
C. Candlemas Day
D. Mardi Gras

Ans: B
Diff: E
Page: 327

46. Contrast the theories of Howard Clark Kee, Michael Mann, and Edward Gibbon which attempt to explain the success of Christianity. Whose position do you find the most convincing? Explain.

Diff: H
Page: 330

47. Monasteries:
A. usually contained members who were celibate
B. were often located in urban areas
C. tended to be complex political organizations
D. were, after the Council of Nicea, exclusively for men

89

Ans: A
Diff: E
Page: 333

48. Eastern Orthodoxy
A. has a different set of scriptures than does Roman Catholicism
B. had a stronger urban base when compared to Roman Catholicism
C. stresses the importance of papal infallibility
D. was strongest in Western Europe

Ans: B
Diff: H
Page: 335

49. This was the strongest Christian denomination in Egypt a thousand years ago:
A. Celtic church
B. Catholic church
C. Coptic church
D. Orthodox church

Ans: C
Diff: M
Page: 336

50. In the eighth century, the advance of Islam into Europe was:
A. most rapid in Scandinavia
B. stopped in southern France by Charles Martel
C. most rapid in Italy
D. of little consequence for the Catholic Church

Ans: B
Diff: M
Page: 338

51. Charlemagne:
A. was crowned Roman Emperor by the Pope
B. suffered several defeats which cut the size of his empire by half
C. was a great friend of the Eastern emperor in Constantinople
D. was the major reason why Europe entered the Dark Ages

Ans: A
Diff: E
Page: 339

52. From 600 C.E. to 1100 C.E., the most fundamental institution in Europe for maintaining order and character was the:
A. monarchy
B. guilds
C. church
D. aristocracy

Ans: C
Diff: M
Page: 341

53. T F Between 500 and 1000 C.E., the church's power was fragmented and decentralized.

Ans: T
Diff: E
Page: 333

54. T F Icons have been more important for Eastern Orthodoxy than for Roman Catholicism.

Ans: T
Diff: E
Page: 335

55. T F The Eastern emperor in Constantinople never acknowledged Charlemagne's title of Holy Roman Emperor.

Ans: F
Diff: E
Page: 341

56. How did the Muslim conquests in western Europe effect the spread of Christianity?

Diff: M
Page: 336

57. What issues and practices acted to bring Eastern Orthodoxy and Roman Catholicism closer together? What issues and practices acted to drive these two branches of Christianity farther apart?

Diff: M
Pages: 335-341

58. Which of the following areas was NOT a major area of strength for Roman Catholicism in the year 1200?
A. Kievan Russia
B. Italy
C. France
D. Germany

Ans: A
Diff: E
Page: 337

59. T F Charlemagne offered Harun-al-Rashid, Caliph of Baghdad, a choice of conversion to Christianity or death.

Ans: F
Diff: M
Page: 339

60. T F The Carolingian Empire was first divided by the Treaty of Verdun in 843 C.E.

Ans: T
Diff: E
Page: 339

1. Muslims believe that the last prophet was:
A. Jesus
B. Muhammad
C. Abraham
D. Abu Bakr

Ans: B
Diff: E
Page: 345

2. Islam:
A. means ascension in Arabic
B. believes in the Holy Trinity
C. places little importance on stories of Muhammad's life
D. believes God transmitted the truth to Muslims through the angel Gabriel

Ans: D
Diff: E
Page: 347

3. Of the following, which is NOT one of the five pillars of Islam?
A. observing a day of rest one day a week
B. praying five times a day while facing Mecca
C. donating alms to the poor
D. making a pilgrimage to Mecca at least once

Ans: A
Diff: E
Pages: 347, 349

4. The Quran promises a reward in paradise to those who
A. make the *haji* at least once
B. observe Islam faithfully
C. dedicate themselves to *jihad*
D. fast during Ramadan

Ans: B
Diff: M
Page: 349

5. Muslims begin their calendar with this event:
A. the birth of Abraham
B. the birth of Muhammad
C. the death of Muhammad
D. the date Muhammad moved to Medina

Ans: D
Diff: M
Page: 350

6. T F During the rule of Umar I, the written and oral recitations of Muhammad were recorded as the Quran.

Ans: T
Diff: E
Page: 347

7. T F The "sixth pillar" of Islam is the *Jihad.*

Ans: T
Diff: E
Page: 349

8. T F According to the Quran, Muhammad was the originator of a new religious doctrine.

Ans: F
Diff: M
Page: 351

9. Define these terms: Quran, hadith, umma, hijra, hajj, Ramadan, Allah, jihad, dar al-Islam.

Diff: M
Pages: 345-354

10. Write an essay that describes the life of the prophet Muhammad from his early meditative days through his success in promulgating Islam.

Diff: M
Pages: 346-347

11. First present the five pillars of Islam, and then discuss the different interpretations of the sixth pillar, the jihad.

Diff: M
Pages: 347-349

12. Which of the following occurred first?
A. the formulation of major systems of Islamic law
B. Ibn Ishaq wrote the biography of Muhammad
C. the Muslims conquer Mecca
D. Baghdad was founded

Ans: C
Diff: M
Page: 346

13. Which of the following has NOT added to the problems of studying Islamic history?
A. the writing of the Quran
B. the writing of the hadith
C. commercial and governmental documents of Islamic societies
D. potential biases of Islamic histories

Ans: C
Diff: M
Page: 350

14. Shari'a:
A. provides rights for men, but not for women
B. specifies that the dowry shall go to the bride's family
C. requires a husband to take care of his children
D. prevents a man from taking more than one wife

15. T F As Ibn Battuta discovered, the status of women in the Islamic world of the fourteenth century was nearly the same everywhere.

16. Abu Bakr:
A. was a direct descendent of Muhammad
B. was the first caliph
C. refused to use force to keep recent converts faithful to Islam
D. ruled for nearly 30 years

17. Of the following, which was the least important motivating factor behind the military expansion of the Islamic Empire?
A. religious goals
B. political goals
C. economic goals
D. military goals

18. The Shi'as:
A. wanted the caliph to focus on imperial aspirations
B. are currently the majority of the Islamic world
C. thought that descendants of Ali should be imam
D. were most numerous in Egypt

19. Mu'awiya:
A. was the first caliph of the Umayyad dynasty
B. was appointed to his post by Muhammad
C. was amateurish in his administration of the empire
D. moved the capital from Arabia to Baghdad

20. The Abbasid caliphate:
A. instituted Persian as the official language of the empire
B. sought to convert non-Muslims to Islam
C. were overthrown by the Umayyads
D. relocated the capital to Damascus in Syria

Ans: B
Diff: M
Page: 359

21. Islamic law:
A. is known in Arabic as the dar al-Islam
B. stays out of daily personal activities
C. consists of two major systems practiced in different regions of the Islamic world
D. is interpreted by *qadis*

Ans: D
Diff: H
Page: 359

22. T F A majority of the first eleven imams were assassinated.

Ans: T
Diff: M
Page: 356

23. T F The Dome of the Rock is one of Islam's most famous mosques.

Ans: T
Diff: M
Page: 356

24. T F The Abbasid clan were descended from Muhammad's uncle.

Ans: T
Diff: E
Page: 359

25. T F The Seljuk Turks abolished the position of caliph.

Ans: F
Diff: M
Page: 360

26. Describe the origins of the divisions between the Sunni and the Shi'a.

Diff: M
Pages: 355-357

27. Compare and contrast the Umayyad caliphate and the Abbasid caliphate in regards to the following: imperial expansion and/or contraction, nature of rule, treatment of non-Muslims, and method of demise.

Diff: H
Pages: 357-359

28. Which of the following regions had NOT yet been conquered by Islam in 650 C.E.?
A. Oman
B. Egypt
C. Spain
D. Libya

Ans: C
Diff: M
Page: 354

29. T F Between 1070 and 1180 C.E., the Abbasid Caliphate lost territory to the Byzantine Empire.

Ans: F
Diff: M
Page: 360

30. The campaigns of Genghis Khan extended as far west as:
A. Kaifeng
B. Liegnitz
C. Ain Jalut
D. the Caucasus Mountains

Ans: D
Diff: M
Page: 361

31. Sufis:
A. are responsible for determining the obligations members of society have to each other
B. were eventually expelled from most Islamic states
C. seek the mystical path to God
D. did not allow aspects of other religions to influence their thought and practices

Ans: C
Diff: M
Page: 368

32. Rumi:
A. thought it was possible to grow closer to God through dance
B. frowned on the writing or reading of inspirational poetry
C. was a famous nineteenth-century Sufi
D. developed a synthesis of the formal and mystical aspects of Islam

Ans: A
Diff: M
Page: 370

33. Ibn Khaldun held all of the following views, except:
A. nomadic peoples tended to conquer urban peoples
B. the only differences between Westerners and Easterners are cultural, not innate
C. scholars are often the wisest rulers
D. tensions between peoples is often related to class

Ans: C
Diff: H
Page: 371

34. The Mutazilites held all of the following views, except:
A. some of the teachings of the Quran were metaphorical, not literal
B. human actions are pre-determined
C. philosophical knowledge can be higher than the revelations of God
D. the Quran had not always existed

Ans: B
Diff: H
Page: 372

35. Use of the decimal system and the zero was first developed by the:
A. Indians
B. Arabs
C. Turks
D. Greeks

Ans: A
Diff: M
Page: 372

36. Many of the major agricultural exchanges that helped the Islamic world came from:
A. sub-Saharan Africa
B. the Fertile Crescent
C. India
D. coastal eastern Africa

Ans: C
Diff: E
Page: 372

37. Baghdad was:
A. once the largest city in the world
B. built near the delta of the Tigris and Euphrates rivers
C. built by the Abbasid dynasty
D. built around 942

Ans: C
Diff: M
Page: 373

38. T F The cnd of the caliphate effectively ended the spread of Islam.

Ans: F
Diff: E
Page: 363

39. T F Sufis were less likely than *ulama* to emphasize strict religious doctrine.

Ans: T
Diff: M
Page: 368

40. T F Muslims repudiated the classical works of Greece and India.

Ans: F
Diff: M
Page: 371

41. Describe the nature and administration of Islamic law. Include a discussion of the *ulama* and the various functions they performed.

Diff: M
Page: 367

42. Write an essay that examines the major accomplishments of Islamic scholars in the fields of history, philosophy, mathematics and science. Did Islamic governments encourage or discourage such scholarly activities?

Diff: H
Pages: 370-372

43. T F Timur's campaigns led as far south as the Sultanate of Delhi

Ans: T
Diff: E
Page: 362

44. T F It wasn't until the mid-fourteenth century that Muslim control extended throughout Deccan.

Ans: T
Diff: M
Page: 363

45. T F Malaysia and Indonesia were relatively late converts to Islam.

Ans: T
Diff: M
Page: 364

46. T F Arab traders brought Islam with them to sub-Saharan Africa.

Ans: T
Diff: E
Page: 366

47. Abu Hamid Muhammad al-Ghazzali:
A. had completed his most important work by the time he was in his early twenties
B. refused to be involved with formal educational institutions
C. saw intellect as one stage of human development
D. felt that rationality was the way to God

Ans: C
Diff: H
Page: 369

48. The crusades:
A. were motivated primarily by religion
B. occurred because the Muslim rulers of Jerusalem prohibited Christian worship there
C. initially went well for the Christians
D. demonstrated the highly civilized nature of Europeans

Ans: C
Diff: M
Page: 377

49. Muslim rule in Spain:
A. was characterized by suppression of Christianity and Judaism
B. extended for nearly 100 years after the rule of Ferdinand and Isabella
C. was tightly controlled by the Abbasid caliph
D. revitalized trade in the western Mediterranean

Ans: D
Diff: M
Page: 378

50. The Alhambra is in this city:
A. Baghdad
B. Damascus
C. Istanbul
D. Granada

Ans: D
Diff: E
Page: 364

51. The Spanish Inquisition was established to:
A. hunt down those suspected of being insincere converts
B. drive paganism out of Spain
C. torture Jews and Muslims
D. counteract the Protestant Reformation

Ans: A
Diff: M
Page: 379

52. Which of the following religions is primarily identified with Indian subcontinent?
A. Islam
B. Buddhism
C. Hinduism
D. Christianity

Ans: B
Diff: M
Page: 381

53. T F *Dhimmi* was the second-class status offered to non-Muslims in areas controlled by Islamic governments

Ans: T
Diff: M
Page: 376

54. T F At one point during the crusades, the Christian invaders killed every Muslim in Jerusalem.

Ans: T
Diff: E
Page: 377

55. T F The *reconquista* of Spain by the Christians was largely complete by the twelfth century.

Ans: F
Diff: M
Page: 379

56. T F By the fourteenth century, Jews and Muslims in Spain were forced to accept baptism and convert to Christianity.

Ans: T
Diff: E
Page: 379

57. First describe the motivations of the Christian crusaders. Next describe their activities, including how civilians were affected, and the ultimate outcome of the endeavor.

Diff: M
Page: 377

58. Islam ruled in Spain for nearly 800 years. Describe the rise and fall of this rule, and discuss important social, political, and economic characteristics of Islamic Spain.

Diff: M
Pages: 378-379

59. T F During the Children's Crusade of 1212 C.E., many were sold as slaves or died of disease and malnutrition.

Ans: T
Diff: E
Page: 377

60. Islam was spread by a variety of means, both peaceful and violent. Which method do you feel was the most effective? Why?

Diff: M
Page: 380

1. According to the text, which of the following is NOT one of the three oldest centers of urban civilization?
A. Mesopotamia
B. the Indus Valley
C. the Nile Valley
D. the Mississippi Valley

Ans: D
Diff: E
Page: 388

2. In a capitalist system, the exchange of goods and services is governed by
A. levels of supply and demand in markets
B. rules which ensure reciprocity between the economic classes
C. laws designed to enhance laissez faire policies
D. a barter system

Ans: A
Diff: M
Page: 389

3. T F By the twelfth century C.E., global trade networks were fully unified.

Ans: F
Diff: M
Page: 388

4. T F Trade routes helped to spread Buddhism and Islam throughout Asia

Ans: T
Diff: E
Page: 388

5. Explain the connection between trade and the spread of epidemics.

Diff: M
Page: 288

6. Photography was invented in the
A. 1860s
B. 1830s
C. 1910s
D. 1750s

Ans: B
Diff: E
Page: 516

7. In 1775, Britain annexed which of the following to its empire in India:
A. Kambia
B. Delhi
C. Baneras
D. Congo

Ans: C
Diff: E
Page: 516

8. T F Slavery was abolished in Europe and European controlled areas in the nineteenth century.

Ans: T
Diff: E
Page: 516

9. T F Slavery was universally condemned in the nineteenth century.

Ans: F
Diff: M
Page: 516

10. "Progress" is often depicted by images of commerce and technology. Is economic development always "progress?" Examine the impact of the rubber industry on workers in the Congo.

Diff: M
Page: 517

1. In the early days of international trade, the most common type of goods was:
A. luxury items
B. processed foods
C. grains
D. metallurgical products

Ans: A
Diff: E
Page: 391

2. Before 1500 C.E., the greatest part of the exchange economy consisted of:
A. long-distance transactions
B. medium-distance transactions
C. local transactions
D. international trade

Ans: C
Diff: E
Page: 391

3. True free market economies require all of the following, except:
A. individuals seeking personal profit
B. benevolent government regulation
C. no control of prices of goods
D. no regulation of demand for goods

Ans: B
Diff: E
Page: 392

4. Which of the following were networks of interconnected commercial communities throughout Africa, Europe and Asia?
A. market centers
B. commercial complexes
C. trade diasporas
D. trade associations

Ans: C
Diff: E
Page: 393

5. During the height of the Roman Empire traders were usually:
A. Jews, Greek-speaking Egyptians, and Arabs
B. ethnically Roman
C. ethnically Germanic
D. Christians

Ans: A
Diff: E
Page: 394

6. T F Market-based economies have always been a part of the exchange of goods and services.

Ans: F
Diff: E
Page: 393

7. Trade in the early societies of Egypt, Mesopotamia, and China, was highly regulated

Ans: T
Diff: E
Page: 393

8. T F Due to their international connections, foreign merchants in port cities tended to occupy central positions in the host society.

Ans: F
Diff: M
Page: 393

9. What are the basic requirements for the functioning of a free market economy?

Diff: M
Page: 392

10. What is the historic root of much of the current resistance to the globalization of trade?

Diff: M
Page: 392

11. T F Marco Polo arrived in China during the Ming dynasty.

Ans: F
Diff: M
Page: 392

12. T F By 1400 C.E. the Arab trading zone included the Americas.

Ans: F
Diff: M
Page: 393

13. The early-fifteenth-century Incas:
A. traded with the Aztec Empire
B. practiced metallurgy primarily in the valleys
C. grew crops on high mountain slopes
D. engaged in a substantial amount of trade, but it was regulated by the government

Ans: D
Diff: M
Page: 396

14. Of the following regions, which had the least extensive network of trade routes in 1450?
A. North America
B. Europe
C. the Middle East
D. southern Asia

Ans: A
Diff: M
Page: 397

15. West African trade:
A. is extensively documented for the period from about 200 C.E. to about 700 C.E.
B. was dependent upon the camel to deliver goods to Europe
C. was centered in Great Zimbabwe
D. was conducted primarily by sailing ship

Ans: B
Diff: M
Page: 397

16. In the year 1350, the majority of gold in circulation in the Middle East came from:
A. the New World
B. the Ural Mountains
C. West Africa
D. Egypt

Ans: C
Diff: E
Page: 399

17. After the ninth century, Arabs provided the main trading link between East Africa and
A. the Indian Ocean
B. the Europe
C. the Americas
D. West Africa

Ans: A
Diff: M
Page: 399

18. Muslim traders:
A. usually stayed out of the Indian Ocean
B. were discouraged from their trade by the Islamic religion
C. eventually ranged as far as China
D. were unsuccessful in planting their religion in the regions in which they traded

Ans: C
Diff: H
Page: 401

19. T F The Aztec government believed in government regulation of the market place.

Ans: T
Diff: E
Page: 396

20. T F The Aztecs and the Mayas worked cooperatively in a Mesoamerican trade network.

Ans: F
Diff: M
Page: 396

21. T F Slaves were an important commodity in East Africa.

Ans: T
Diff: E
Page: 400

22. T F The Jewish trading community linked Europe and Asia.

Ans: T
Diff: E
Page: 400

23. Discuss the nature and importance of trade in the Americas in the 1400s.

Diff: H
Pages: 394-397

24. Write an essay on West Africa and East Africa trade in the 1400s that includes discussion of main routes, how goods were transported, and what the principle goods were.

Diff: M
Pages: 397-400

25. The Incas used which of the following to record dates and accounts?
A. beads
B. tablets
C. *quipu*
D. *pochteca*

Ans: C
Diff: E
Page: 394

26. T F The Mayas dominated the Yucatán peninsula through 900 C.E.

Ans: T
Diff: M
Page: 395

27. The three largest West African empires were:
A. Ghana, Takrur, Mali
B. Mali, Songhay, Ghana
C. Funj, Ethiopia, Adal
D. Kongo, Zimbabwe, Bagirmi

Ans: B
Diff: M
Page: 398

28. T F The documents from the Cairo Genizah contain several manuscripts written by women in the Jewish community.

Ans: F
Diff: M
Page: 402

29. The primary focus of Polynesian sailors was
A. to explore the Pacific Ocean
B. to establish a trade system throughout the Pacific
C. to locate new places in which to settle
D. to establish an empire in the Pacific

Ans: C
Diff: M
Page: 403

30. The primary focus of Malay sailors was
A. to explore the Indian Ocean
B. to establish sea routs from East Africa to China
C. to locate new places in which to settle
D. to establish an empire in the Indian Ocean

Ans: B
Diff: M
Page: 404

31. During which dynasty did China overthrow the Mongols?
A. Song
B. Ming
C. Tang
D. Qing

Ans: B
Diff: E
Page: 408

32. During the Tang dynasty, Chinese trade activity increased in:
A. the South China Sea and the Pacific Ocean
B. the Arabian Sea and the Indian Ocean
C. the South China Sea and the Indian Ocean
D. the Java Sea and the Arabian Sea

Ans: C
Diff: E
Page: 408

33. Chinese luxury products included tea, silk and
A. linen
B. porcelain
C. paper
D. spices

Ans: B
Diff: E
Page: 412

34. T F In 1500 internal Chinese trade was much more significant than its external trade.

Ans: T
Diff: E
Page: 408

35. T F The Ming government prohibited private overseas trade by Chinese merchants.

Ans: T
Diff: E
Page: 410

36. T F The Grand Canal connected the agricultural region in the west with the administrative centers in the south.

Ans: F
Diff: M
Page: 414

37. Discuss and analyze the impact of the decline of the Tang dynasty on international trade.

Diff: M
Pages: 408-409

38. Discuss and analyze the consequences of the trade policies of the Ming dynasty.

Diff: H
Pages: 410-411

39. Which of the following trading ports and cities in the Indian Ocean declined in prominence after 1000 C.E.?
A. Zanzibar
B. Delhi
C. Calicut
D. Kanchipura

Ans: D
Diff: M
Page: 405

40. The Bay of Bengal trade region included which of the following ports?
A. Hai-nan
B. Aden
C. Cambay
D. Hormuz

Ans: C
Diff: M
Page: 406

41. Describe the ways in which Sinbad's adventures reflect the realities of international trade in the Indian Ocean.

Diff: M
Page: 407

42. Based on Ibn Battuta's account, describe Chinese attitudes toward foreigners in the 1300s.
Diff: M
Page: 410

43. According the Marco Polo, Pao Hui and Xu Xianzhong, describe the ways in which common people contributed to the silk trade.

Diff: M
Page: 413

44. Prior to 1200, the Mongols:
A. prohibited the silk trade
B. were divided into several warring tribes
C. were primarily farmers
D. were never united prior to the time of Genghis Khan

Ans: B
Diff: M
Page: 414

45. Marco Polo supposedly did all of the following, except:
A. travel to China
B. travel to southern Africa
C. dictate his memoirs
D. land in jail

Ans: B
Diff: E
Page: 416

46. Chinggis Khan:
A. would not have agreed with the theories of Machiavelli
B. was at the height of his power around the year 1338
C. adopted Chinese siege methods
D. was born into a lower-class family

Ans: C
Diff: M
Page: 417

47. Chinggis and his successors were NOT able to conquer:
A. Japan
B. China
C. Russia
D. Baghdad

Ans: A
Diff: E
Page: 418

48. The rule of the Mongols was relatively brief largely because:
A. their empire was too extensive for them to rule it effectively
B. Genghis Khan's sons immediately fought each other after his death
C. most Mongols were wiped out by the bubonic plague
D. they were often unwilling to use force against opponents

Ans: A
Diff: H
Page: 419

49. The bubonic plague:
A. is transmitted by flies
B. was spread primarily due to the activities of the Mongols
C. had less effect in Europe than in other places where the disease struck
D. never reached China

Ans: B
Diff: M
Page: 419

50. T F At its height, the Mongol Empire was the largest empire the world had yet known.

Ans: T
Diff: M
Page: 419

51. T F Under the leadership of Chinggis, the Mongols developed a new legal code which called for high moral standards.

Ans: T
Diff: M
Page: 417

52. T F During years of Mongol control China experienced a population increase of 50%.

Ans: F
Diff: M
Page: 420

53. Describe the extent of the Mongol Empire at its height. How did the Mongols manage to conquer so many people?

Diff: M
Pages: 414-418

54. Identify and explain the main reason for the dissolution of the Mongol empire? What happened to the Mongols afterward?

Diff: M
Page: 419

55. Explain why it is necessary for scholars to understand Chinese, Persian, Arabic, Turkish, Japanese, Russian, Armenian, Georgian, and Latin in order to study the Mongols.

Diff: M
Page: 415

56. Which of the following Mongol states encompassed Tibet?
A. Khanate of the Golden Horde
B. Il-Khan Empire
C. Empire of the Great Khan
D. Chagatai Empire

Ans: C
Diff: E
Page: 418

57. T F The Black Death, or bubonic plague, originated in Central Asia.

Ans: T
Diff: E
Page: 420

1. Permanent contact between Europe and the Americas did NOT occur until
A. 1533 C.E.
B. 1000 C.E.
C. 1492 C.E.
D. 870 C.E.

Ans: C
Diff: E
Page: 425

2. Leif Eriksson led the Vikings established a settlement in North America around
A. 500 C.E.
B. 1000 C.E.
C. 982 C.E.
D. 870 C.E.

Ans: B
Diff: E
Page: 425

3. William of Normandy led the Vikings to conquer which country in 1066?
A. England
B. Sicily
C. Italy
D. Ireland

Ans: A
Diff: E
Page: 426

4. Which of the following controlled the northeastern shores of the Mediterranean in 1000 C.E.
A. Muslims
B. Byzantine Empire
C. Frankish and Germanic Christian
D. the Mongols

Ans: B
Diff: M
Page: 427

5. The contest for control of the Mediterranean was primary the result of
A. religious differences
B. competition for profit
C. ethnic differences
D. political differences

Ans: B
Diff: M
Page: 429

6. T F Except for the Viking excursions, voyages across the north Atlantic are unlikely to have occurred.

Ans: T
Diff: E
Page: 426

7. T F The Mediterranean was divided into two major cultural and political spheres of control: Muslim and Byzantine.

Ans: F
Diff: M
Page: 427

8. T F Due to devastation from the plague, European trade did not begin to recover until the early fifteenth century.

Ans: T
Diff: M
Page: 429

9. Describe the factors that led Europeans to begin exploring for new routes to major trade markets.

Diff: M
Page: 425

10. Explain the political and cultural divisions of the Mediterranean circa 1000 C.E.

Diff: M
Pages: 426-427

11. T F The Vikings were most active in north western Europe.

Ans: T
Diff: M
Page: 427

12. Which of the following occurred first?
A. Bubonic Plague in Europe
B. Normans invaded England
C. Great Chinese naval expeditions to Africa and India
D. Magellen's circumnavigation of the globe

Ans: B
Diff: M
Page: 428

13. T F Warfare between Christians and Muslims continued in the Mediterranean until 1571.

Ans: T
Diff: E
Page: 429

14. In the 1300s and 1400s, guilds:
A. represented both artisans and unskilled workers
B. successfully agitated for a voice in city government
C. were usually led by rural aristocrats
D. made it difficult for prosperous cities to assert their independence

Ans: B
Diff: M
Page: 430

15. The economies of north Italy and Flanders were dominated by which of the following?
A. silk production
B. ship building
C. textiles manufacturing
D. timber industry

Ans: C
Diff: E
Page: 430

16. According to historians of the Church, the roots of the Renaissance can be found as early as:
A. the fourteenth century
B. the mid-eleventh century
C. the thirteenth century
D. the fifteenth century

Ans: B
Diff: M
Page: 433

17. Which of the following was NOT the emphasis of most early universities?
A. military history
B. medicine
C. legal studies
D. theology

Ans: A
Diff: M
Pages: 433-434

18. Which of the following was NOT one of the disasters that afflicted fourteenth and fifteenth century Europe?
A. famine
B. plague
C. civil upheavals
D. drought

Ans: D
Diff: M
Page: 436

19. In the fourteenth and fifteenth centuries:
A. Europe's population nearly doubled
B. peasants who survived the plague often found their situation improved
C. France and England remained at peace
D. the Renaissance became most strongly entrenched among the lower classes

Ans: B
Diff: M
Page: 437

20. T F Guilds strictly regulated the prices of their products.

Ans: T
Diff: E
Page: 430

21. T F According to St. Thomas Aquinas, Aristotelian logic undermined the teachings of the Church.

Ans: F
Diff: M
Page: 434

22. T F The Ciompi in Florence revolted and in 1378 demanded the right to unionize.

Ans: T
Diff: M
Page: 437

23. In the eleventh century, philosophers proposed that pure faith was not enough to attain salvation. Explain what changes they sought to evoke.

Diff: M
Page: 433

24. Describe the impact of the plague on the conditions of laborers at the end of the fourteenth century. In what ways did it lead to improved conditions?

Diff: M
Page: 437

25. The *Annales* school of history:
A. was named for a Parisian café frequented by French historians: the Café des Annales
B. was centered in the University of Paris
C. published a journal edited by historians for historians
D. emphasized an interdisciplinary approach to history

Ans: D
Diff: M
Page: 431

26. What were the important contributions to the study of history made by the *Annales* school, especially Fernand Braudel and his use of three time frames of history?

Diff: M
Page: 454

27. Explain the Arabic influence on the European Renaissance. What would you say was their most significant contribution?

Diff: M
Page: 435

28. According to Giovanni Boccaccio, in what way did the plague affect traditional family relationships?

Diff: M
Page: 437

29. During the Renaissance, European artists began to utilize which of the following in their paintings?
A. acrylic paint
B. perspective
C. Arabic themes
D. Asian themes

Ans: B
Diff: D
Page: 438

30. Which of the following is an Arabic invention that aided in commercial navigation during the fifteenth century?
A. the sextant
B. the barometer
C. the astrolabe
D. the compass

Ans: C
Diff: M
Page: 441

31. Which of the following is an Chinese invention utilized by Europeans to conquer countries and dominate trade routes.
A. gunpowder
B. cannons
C. catapults
D. caravels

Ans: A
Diff: M
Page: 441

32. In the high Middle Ages, most European Jews:
A. were forbidden to loan money
B. lived freely among Christians
C. were often successful traders
D. sought to return to ancient Israel and Judea

Ans: C
Diff: E
Page: 441

33. As expressed in Aquinas' *Summa Theologica*, the Church began to modify its traditional opposition towards:
A. Jews
B. business and businessmen
C. Muslims
D. women

Ans: B
Diff: M
Page: 442

34. T F Humanism is the belief that the proper study of man is man.

Ans: T
Diff: E
Page: 438

35. T F Masaccio's *Trinity with the Virgin* demonstrates the use of perspective in painting.

Ans: T
Diff: E
Pages: 438-439

36. T F Although the Chinese invented the principle of movable type, the Arabs perfected it.

Ans: F
Diff: M
Page: 441

37. Explain the impact of humanism on Christian beliefs in the fifteenth century.

Diff: M
Page: 438

38. Describe the factors that influenced the Church to re-evaluate commerce in the fifteenth century. What was the new position of the Church on business?

Diff: M
Page: 442

39. T F Florence is at the center of the Italian intellectual movement that ushered in the Renaissance.

Ans: T
Diff: M
Page: 438

40. Prince Henry the Navigator established a center for the study of navigation in order to:
A. discover new lands
B. chart the oceans
C. control the eastern coast of Africa
D. end Muslim control of the southern shores of the Mediterranean

Ans: D
Diff: E
Page: 442

41. Christopher Columbus initially sought support for his expedition from:
A. Spain
B. Italy
C. Portugal
D. France

Ans: C
Diff: M
Page: 444

42. Which of the following explorers was the first to clearly recognize that Columbus had NOT discovered a route to Asia?
A. Vasco de Gama
B. Amerigo Vespucci
C. Vasco Nuñez de Balboa
D. Bartolomeo Dias

Ans: B
Diff: E
Page: 445

43. Which of the following explorers crossed the Isthmus of Panama and became the first European to see the Pacific Ocean?
A. Vasco de Gama
B. Amerigo Vespucci
C. Vasco Nuñez de Balboa
D. Bartolomeo Dias

Ans: C
Diff: E
Page: 445

44. The sea voyages of exploration and discovery:
A. included the first round-the-world voyage by Ferdinand Magellan in the first half of the sixteenth century
B. were spearheaded by the prosperous Italian city-states
C. began with Columbus' discovery of America
D. were financed in large part by the Ottoman Empire

Ans: A
Diff: E
Page: 446

45. T F The Portuguese constructed caravels based on Arab ship and sail designs.

Ans: T
Diff: E
Page: 443

46. T F Prince Henry the Navigator was an early supporter of Christopher Columbus.

Ans: F
Diff: E
Page: 444

47. T F On his death bed, Christopher Columbus finally realized the enormity of his discovery.

Ans: F
Diff: E
Page: 445

48. Describe the innovations in navigation and ship design introduced by experts gathered by Prince Henry the Navigator. How did these innovations affect the role of Portugal in international exploration?

Diff: M
Pages: 443-444

49. List and examine the different motives for the fifteenth century voyages of exploration.

Diff: M
Page: 447

50. Which of the following explorers did NOT cross the Atlantic?
A. Coelho and Vespucci
B. Columbus
C. Magellan
D. Dias

Ans: D
Diff: M
Page: 443

Part 5: The Movement of Goods and Peoples (1000 – 1776)
Chapter 14: The Unification of World Trade (1500 – 1776)

1. Which of the following statements about Spain's conquests in the New World is NOT true?
A. Columbus made four voyages to the New World
B. Hernán Cortés overthrew the Aztec empire
C. Spanish settlers first colonized the Pacific coast of South America
D. Francisco Pizarro murdered the Inca emperor

Ans: C
Diff: M
Page: 452

2. Which of the following is NOT a reason why the Spaniards were able to defeat much larger Native American forces?
A. The natives lacked the will to fight
B. The natives were divided amongst themselves
C. The natives lacked the technology of the Spaniards
D. The natives were devastated by European diseases

Ans: A
Diff: M
Page: 454

3. Spain's most valuable exports from the Americas in the sixteenth century were:
A. beef products
B. silver and gold
C. wool and cotton
D. agricultural foodstuffs

Ans: B
Diff: M
Page: 457

4. Portugal:
A. has been independent for over 1000 years
B. had little success in world trade
C. had insufficient population to maintain a trading empire
D. was a late-comer to world trade

Ans: C
Diff: M
Page: 461

5. Which of the following was NOT one of the countries that surpassed Spain and Portugal as economic and political powers by the end of the sixteenth century?
A. Netherlands
B. France
C. Italy
D. England

Ans: C
Diff: E
Page: 462

6. T F The *encomienda* system failed when the Indian population was decimated by disease and cruelty.

Ans: T
Diff: M
Page: 457

7. T F The Portuguese built fortresses, such as El Mina, as shipping points for their purchases of slaves and gold.

Ans: T
Diff: E
Page: 459

8. T F With the wealth gained from its conquests in America, Spain remained the dominant European power well into the eighteenth century.

Ans: F
Diff: M
Page: 462

9. Describe the different types of economic organization used by the Spaniards in the Americas. Were some more exploitative than others?

Diff: M
Page: 457

10. Explain why Spain and Portugal failed to sustain the wealth they amassed through exploration in the sixteenth century.

Diff: M
Page: 462

11. Adam Smith felt that:
A. mercantilism was the best way to make a country economically powerful
B. if workers specialized in tasks they performed well, the economy would be more productive
C. governments should provide only for the defense of the country and the punishment of criminals
D. business profits should be used to buy imports

Ans: B
Diff: M
Page: 453

12. Adam Smith felt that wealth is created by:
A. the command of kings
B. the urgings of religious leaders
C. altruistic actions of citizens
D. the pursuit of economic self-interest

Ans: D
Diff: E
Page: 453

13. T F Adam Smith knew that the free market would NOT always adequately balance supply and demand.

Ans: T
Diff: H
Page: 453

14. T F Pizarro's conquest of the Inca empire occurred ten years before Cortés and conquered the Aztec empire.

Ans: F
Diff: M
Page: 455

15. T F Portuguese possessions in the Americas are located primarily in the northern hemisphere.

Ans: F
Diff: E
Page: 456

16. T F By 1750, major trade routes connected the Americas with Africa, Europe, Asia, and the Pacific islands.

Ans: T
Diff: E
Page: 459

17. This event established and sanctioned the split between Catholic and Protestant countries in Europe:
A. Thirty Years War
B. the Edict of Nantes
C. French Wars of Religion
D. Council of Trent

Ans: A
Diff: M
Page: 463

18. Martin Luther:
A. was an upper class German businessman
B. approved of the selling of indulgences
C. urged the suppression of a peasant revolt in Germany
D. eventually became the Pope

Ans: C
Diff: E
Page: 463

19. This person believed in predestination and set up a theocracy in Switzerland:
A. Martin Luther
B. Ulrich Zwingli
C. Jan Hus
D. John Calvin

Ans: D
Diff: M
Page: 465

20. In the 1500s and early 1600s, the Netherlands:
A. stayed loyal to their rulers
B. refused to give in to Protestant sentiment
C. agitated for independence
D. stayed aloof from England

Ans: C
Diff: M
Page: 466

21. Queen Elizabeth of England:
A. never strayed from the Catholic faith
B. won a war with Spain
C. refused to help the Netherlands
D. was the mother of Henry the VIII

Ans: B
Diff: E
Page: 466

22. The Dutch Republic in the seventeenth century:
A. relied on agriculture as the mainstay of the economy
B. was unable to win independence from Spain
C. fought a costly war with Russia
D. developed innovative methods of crop rotation that boosted agricultural output

Ans: D
Diff: M
Page: 466

23. This country dominated northern European shipping in the seventeenth century:
A. England
B. France
C. Denmark
D. Netherlands

Ans: D
Diff: E
Page: 467

24. In France in the second half of the sixteenth century:
A. there was relative peace
B. nearly all the inhabitants were Catholic
C. Henry IV converted to Catholicism
D. a revolution occurred with the slogan "liberté, egalité, fraternité"

Ans: C
Diff: M
Page: 470

25. Louis the XIV's economic policies:
A. were opposed by Jean-Baptiste Colbert
B. included the abolition of internal tax-free zones
C. prevented any standardization of French business practices
D. included a policy of mercantilism

Ans: D
Diff: M
Page: 470

26. During the eighteenth century, France:
A. had the most powerful navy
B. lost its holdings in North America
C. had a small army in comparison with Britain
D. won a major victory in the Seven Years' War

Ans: B
Diff: E
Page: 472

27. Britain gained supremacy in world trade in part by:
A. having a unified national market
B. spending much of the government's funds on a powerful land army
C. refusing to develop its rivers as transportation systems
D. having a small navy

Ans: A
Diff: H
Page: 472

28. During its period of ascendancy in world trade, Britain did all of the following, except:
A. fix the value of its currency to a set amount of silver
B. create the Bank of England
C. keep separate markets with separate regulations and taxes within Britain
D. institute a system of government that favored private enterprise

Ans: C
Diff: H
Page: 472

29. T F The Netherlands did NOT develop the financial institutions necessary to help them stay an important economic power.

Ans: F
Diff: M
Page: 466

30. T F True to its name, the Dutch East India Company focused its efforts on the eastern portion of India.

Ans: F
Diff: E
Page: 467

31. T F Louis XIV of France thought the king was just "first among equals" within the aristocracy.

Ans: F
Diff: M
Page: 470

32. Discuss the initial spark for the Reformation, and then move on to a description of the three major strands of the movement, and also the counter-Reformation that followed.

Diff: H
Pages: 462-465

33. Why did the Netherlands want independence? How did they gain it?

Diff: M
Page: 466

34. Which of the following remained a Catholic country throughout the Reformation and Counter-Reformation?
A. England
B. France
C. Spain
D. Poland

Ans: C
Diff: M
Page: 463

35. Outline the arguments of Max Weber and R.H. Tawney concerning the relationship between religious doctrine and economic policy. Which do you feel makes the best argument? Why?

Diff: M
Page: 465

36. Using examples, describe the activities of joint stock companies in the seventeenth century. How were such companies founded?

Diff: M
Page: 468

37. Which of the following controlled a trade route that went directly to Java?
A. The Portuguese
B. The Dutch
C. The Spanish
D. The French

Ans: B
Diff: E
Page: 471

38. T F England did not secure its control of India until they subdued the Maratha Confederacy in 1818.

Ans: T
Diff: E
Page: 472

39. The concept of a nation-state does NOT include which of the following?
A. a sense of shared ethnic identity
B. a geographic territory with an independent government
C. a shared language and history
D. a shared sense of unity with surrounding states

Ans: D
Diff: M
Page: 472

40. Which of the following nation-states was governed by a coalition of businessmen?
A. England
B. the Netherlands
C. France
D. Portugal

Ans: B
Diff: E
Page: 473

41. The Russian state did not begin to form until it overthrew
A. Islam domination
B. Ottoman domination
C. Mongol domination
D. Swedish domination

Ans: C
Diff: M
Page: 473

42. Seventeenth-century Russia:
A. was well on its way to becoming a major international economic power
B. had several ports on the Black Sea that operated year round
C. was not able to make use of its rivers for transportation purposes
D. had only a very small urban trading class

Ans: D
Diff: M
Page: 474

43. Peter the Great:
A. saw the Hapsburg empire as his greatest enemy
B. saw Sweden invade his country and capture the western third of it, including Moscow
C. developed new weapons and military tactics without the help of western European ideas
D. made major reforms in administration that made his bureaucracy more efficient

Ans: D
Diff: M
Page: 475

44. T F Nation-states all employed a mercantilist economic policy.

Ans: F
Diff: M
Page: 473

45. T F Peter I hoped to westernize Russia.

Ans: T
Diff: E
Page: 475

46. T F Catherine the Great abolished serfdom in Russia.

Ans: F
Diff: M
Page: 476

47. Explain the impact of world trade on the development of nation states in the sixteenth and seventeenth centuries.

Diff: M
Page: 473

48. Write an essay that presents the reforms and achievements of Peter the Great.

Diff: M
Pages: 474-475

49. By 1725, Peter the Great had extended Russian control to include access to:
A. the Arctic Ocean and the Caspian Sea
B. the Baltic Sea and the Caspian Sea
C. the Black Sea and the Baltic Sea
D. The Black Sea and the Caspian Sea

Ans: C
Diff: M
Page: 474

50. The authority of the Ottoman Empire was undermined in the 1500s in part because of:
A. its political alliance with the Mongols
B. open trade with the English and the Dutch
C. its trade alliance with the Mughal Empire
D. its weak military

Ans: B
Diff: M
Page: 476

51. Akbar, the ruler of India:
A. was head of the Mughal empire
B. turned the cash economy into a barter economy
C. would not allow the installation of a national money system
D. suppressed guilds

Ans: A
Diff: E
Page: 476

52. The Ming dynasty:
A. allowed the Great Wall to fall into disrepair
B. opened China wide to foreign trade
C. fought with Japan during the last decade of the sixteenth century
D. built a powerful navy

Ans: C
Diff: M
Page: 477

53. The Qing dynasty was successful in
A. creating trade networks with European nation-states
B. subduing Japanese efforts to conquer China
C. keeping European merchants out of China
D. completing the Great Wall.

Ans: C
Diff: E
Page: 478

54. Conversion to Christianity was most common among which group in Japan?
A. the warrior class
B. the elite
C. the royal court
D. the peasants

Ans: B
Diff: M
Page: 480

55. T F The Mughal empire encouraged the development of internal trade.

Ans: T
Diff: M
Page: 476

56. T F The Ming dynasty was successful in repelling a Japanese invasion.

Ans: T
Diff: E
Page: 477

57. T F The Tokugawa government of seventeenth century Japan was primarily controlled by the warrior classes.

Ans: T
Diff: E
Page: 480

58. Explain why Indian efforts to engage in coastal and oceanic trade were largely unsuccessful in the sixteenth and seventeenth centuries.

Diff: M
Pages: 476-477

59. How did Tokugawa Japan deal with Christianity and international trade during the sixteenth and seventeenth centuries?

Diff: M
Page: 480

60. Describe the new economic religious philosophies that contributed to the increase in power of the European nation-states.

Diff: M
Page: 481

61. According to economic historians Mark Elvin and Kenneth Pomeranz, why did the economy of China stagnate during the Ming and early Qing dynasties.

Diff: M
Page: 479

1. Demographers are least likely to do the following:
A. study aggregate human populations
B. use statistical analysis
C. interpret patterns of human change
D. do an in-depth study of a single individual

Ans: D
Diff: H
Page: 485

2. Which of the following did NOT move from the Old World to the New World in the Columbian exchange?
A. potatoes
B. sheep
C. wheat
D. horses

Ans: A
Diff: E
Page: 487

3. Which of the following did NOT compete for control in North America?
A. Spain
B. France
C. Dutch Republic
D. Germany

Ans: D
Diff: E
Page: 487

4. Captain James Cook:
A. was an American
B. gave a positive report about Australia
C. was killed in a clash with Tahitian natives
D. had no way of determining his longitude

Ans: B
Diff: E
Page: 492

5. Australia:
A. was initially populated by prisoners
B. has a lush interior
C. has a thriving indigenous population
D. experienced a major gold rush in the 1930s

Ans: A
Diff: E
Page: 492

6. The Maori:
A. are an indigenous tribe in Australia
B. were a pacifistic people
C. saw their population decrease by more than half as a result of interactions with Europeans
D. were given sovereignty over vast tracts of rich territory by the British government

Ans: C
Diff: M
Page: 493

7. T F New World crops helped fuel China's population explosion.

Ans: T
Diff: M
Page: 487

8. T F War with Europeans was the reason for the major decline of the Amerindian population after 1500.

Ans: F
Diff: E
Page: 487

9. T F The Dutch were the first Europeans to settle in South Africa.

Ans: T
Diff: E
Page: 494

10. Briefly describe what demographers study and the tools they use to help them in their tasks.

Diff: M
Page: 485

11. What happened to the Maori people under British rule?

Diff: M
Page: 493

12. Which of the following possessed the most colonies along the Atlantic coast of North America?
A. the French
B. the English
C. the Spanish
D. the Dutch

Ans: B
Diff: E
Page: 488

13. Of the following colonies, which was settled first?
A. Carolina
B. Delaware
C. New York
D. Pennsylvania

Ans: C
Diff: E
Page: 489

14. Contrast William Dampier's view of the Maroi with that of Captain Cook. Explain what you think might have contributed to their different perspectives.

Diff: M
Page: 491

15. Slavery:
A. began when Europeans began taking Africans from the west coast of Africa
B. brought nearly 10 million Africans to the Western Hemisphere
C. was most important for agriculture on and near the east coast of North America
D. was initiated by Spain

Ans: B
Diff: M
Page: 496

16. In which type of agricultural production were slaves most likely to receive the worst treatment?
A. cotton
B. sugar
C. tobacco
D. corn

Ans: B
Diff: M
Page: 497

17. The slave trade:
A. took slaves primarily from the east coast of Africa
B. predominantly served the needs of the North American continent
C. was largely dependent on the activities of native African businessmen
D. did not begin until Europeans desired slaves

Ans: C
Diff: M
Page: 497

18. Of the following, which is NOT one of the reasons that slavery and the slave trade were important to African states?
A. slaves represented the main form of wealth
B. slaves were a source of labor
C. trade in slaves led to increased wealth
D. enslavement offered a way to eliminate members of rival states

Ans: D
Diff: M
Page: 497

19. Which of the following is NOT a reason that Europeans did not venture into the interior of Africa?
A. lack of sufficient military strength
B. susceptibility to disease
C. racist fears concerning Africans
D. lack of knowledge about the terrain

Ans: C
Diff: M
Page: 497

20. T F The Portuguese were the first Europeans to carry the slave trade to the Atlantic coast.

Ans: T
Diff: E
Page: 496

21. T F All African rulers resisted the slave trade.

Ans: F
Diff: E
Page: 497

22. T F Trade in slaves did not become a significant activity in world history until Europeans began engaging in it.

Ans: F
Diff: M
Page: 498

23. First describe the origins of the slave trade. Then compare, contrast, and analyze the roles of Africans and Europeans in the slave trade.

Diff: M
Page: 497

24. Explain why some scholars argue that the slave trade had little effect on the economic and cultural development in Africa. Do you find their arguments convincing?

Diff: M
Page: 499

25. Geographically, which is the largest British colony?
A. Cape Colony
B. Sierra Leone
C. New Zealand
D. Maruitius

Ans: C
Diff: M
Page: 495

26. In the mid-nineteenth century Tasmania was home to four penal colonies.

Ans: T
Diff: E
Page: 495

27. T F The battles of the Maori wars were fought on the North Island of New Zealand.

Ans: T
Diff: E
Page: 495

28. According to Philip Curtin, the Caribbean sugar plantation economy of the 1700s had all of the following characteristics, except:
A. it was a large-scale capitalist enterprise
B. it relied on slave labor
C. political control lay in Europe
D. it produced most of its own food

Ans: D
Diff: M
Page: 498

29. T F The American colonies gained many of their new slaves through natural growth of the existing slave population.

Ans: T
Diff: M
Page: 498

30. Write an essay that describes the key findings of Philip Curtin's investigation into slavery in the Americas, including the sources of slaves, the numbers of slaves, and the nature of the systems that used slaves.

Diff: H
Pages: 498-99

31. This group accompanied Ottoman soldiers to help convert conquered peoples to Islam:
A. Sufis
B. gazis
C. janissaries
D. medresses

Ans: A
Diff: E
Page: 501

32. The Ottoman Empire:
A. won Serbia in the late 1500s
B. converted nearly the entire population of the Balkans to Islam
C. forced most Balkan residents to flee the empire's lands
D. did allow the practice of Christianity in the Balkans

Ans: D
Diff: M
Page: 501

33. Akbar did all of the following except:
A. allow foreigners to serve in his bureaucracy
B. ban use of the Urdu language
C. allow Sufis to preach in Hindi
D. practice syncretism

Ans: B
Diff: M
Page: 504

34. The Mongols who invaded Persia in the thirteenth century:
A. overthrew the Safavid dynasty
B. massacred whole populations of cities
C. did not integrate themselves with local people and practices
D. made no attempt to maintain the area's infrastructure

Ans: B
Diff: M
Page: 505

35. The Qing dynasty:
A. negotiated a border treaty with Russia
B. never managed to gain control of Tibet
C. saw the borders of China contract substantially
D. oversaw a population that stayed about the same size, with minor fluctuations

Ans: A
Diff: M
Page: 507

36. T F In 1530 the Ottoman Empire probably had a larger population than England, Spain, and Portugal combined.

Ans: T
Diff: M
Page: 502

37. T F The Safavid Empire controlled much of modern-day Turkey.

Ans: F
Diff: E
Page: 506

38. T F The Treaty of Nerchinsk was the first Chinese-European treaty negotiated on terms of equality.

Ans: T
Diff: E
Page: 507

39. First describe the geographic extent of the Mughal Empire under Akbar. Then describe and analyze the social, religious, economic, and political characteristics of his rule. Why do some consider him India's greatest ruler?

Diff: H
Page: 507

40. Describe important territorial gains and international agreements of the Qing (Manchu) dynasty.

Diff: M
Page: 507

41. Eurasian empires existing from 1300 to 1700:
A. typically had ocean ports to facilitate trading
B. had buffer states in-between them to help reduce friction
C. were linked by overland trade routes
D. had dynamic bureaucracies that prepared them for the future challenges of Europeans

Ans: C
Diff: M
Page: 500

42. T F Akbar nearly doubled the size of the Mughal Empire by 1609.

Ans: T
Diff: E
Page: 503

43. Which of the following occurred last?
A. the Mayflower set sail for the New World
B. the English founded a colony in Virginia
C. The British annexed New Zealand
D. Akbar established the Mughal Empire

Ans: C
Diff: E
Page: 505

44. Demographers estimate that between 1000 and 1700 the population of Europe:
A. nearly doubled
B. more than tripled
C. more than quadrupled
D. remained steady

Ans: B
Diff: E
Page: 508

45. In the 1600s Akbar's grandson Shah Jahan rebuilt the city of Delhi and renamed it
A. New Delhi
B. Jahangir, after his father
C. Akbarabad, after his grandfather
D. Shahjahanabad, after himself

Ans: D
Diff: M
Page: 509

46. In Iran, Shah Abbas found common ground with the European powers in their mutual opposition to the:
A. Ottoman Empire
B. Mughal Empire
C. Ming dynasty
D. Qing dynasty

Ans: A
Diff: E
Page: 511

47. In 1453 Sultan Mehmed II captured Constantinople and renamed it:
A. New Julfa
B. Shahjahanabad
C. Istanbul
D. Isfahan

Ans: C
Diff: E
Page: 511

48. Of the following cities, which did NOT suffer decline during the seventeenth century?
A. London
B. Peking
C. Delhi
D. Isfahan

Ans: A
Diff: M
Page: 512

49. T F Shah Jahanabad served as a major religious center.

Ans: T
Diff: M
Page: 509

50. T F In 1598, Isfahan was one of the largest cities of its time.

Ans: T
Diff: E
Page: 510

51. T F By the end of the 1600s, the population of London encompassed more than two-thirds of the entire population of England.

Ans: F
Diff: M
Page: 512

52. Contrast the actions of Shah Abbas with the way he was described by friar Paul Simon in a report to Pope Paul V in 1605. What reasons might friar Simon have had in portraying him in this manner?

Diff: H
Page: 511

53. Explain the factors that contributed to growth and development of major cities prior to 1800.

Diff: M
Page: 514

54. According to Ibn Khaldun, what impact did urbanization have on nomadic invaders of a more settled region? Do you find his conclusions convincing?

Diff: M
Page: 510

Part 6: Social Change (1640 – 1914)

1. Global exploration expanded at an unprecedented rate beginning in the
A. thirteenth century
B. seventeenth century
C. tenth century
D. eighteenth century

Ans: A
Diff: E
Page: 518

2. Which of the following was NOT a method of disseminating new political, economic, and social philosophies?
A. political colonialism
B. economic imperialism
C. cultural isolationism
D. missionary activity

Ans: C
Diff: M
Page: 518

3. T F The "Age of Revolution," 1640-1914, includes revolutions in France, Haiti and North America.

Ans: T
Diff: E
Page: 518

4. T F The "Industrial Revolution" had little impact on the institution of the family.

Ans: F
Diff: M
Page: 519

5. Explain why new political, economic, and social philosophies might manifest themselves in different ways in different societies.

Diff: M
Pages: 518-519

6. The breakthrough in gender relations in the Olympics occurred when women were allowed to participate in which of the following events?
A. gymnastics
B. track and field
C. synchronized swimming
D. speed skating

Ans: B
Diff: E
Page: 644

7. Palestinian terrorists murdered two Israeli athletes and seized nine as hostages in the Olympic Games of:
A. 1956
B. 1964
C. 1968
D. 1972

Ans: D
Diff: E
Page: 645

8. T F The new Olympic Games were successful in part due to rampant nationalism at the end of the nineteenth century.

Ans: T
Diff: E
Page: 644

9. T F The Russian invasion of Afghanistan led the United States to boycott the 1980 Olympics in Moscow.

Ans: T
Diff: E
Page: 645

10. Describe how the Second World War affected the Olympic Games of 1940 and 1944.

Diff: M
Page: 645

1. A political revolution:
A. can leave the same people in power at the highest levels
B. is by definition rapid
C. changes the basis on which leaders come to power
D. is necessarily violent

Ans: C
Diff: H
Page: 521

2. The revolutions that occurred between 1688 and 1789:
A. affirmed the divine right of kings
B. limited power to members of the upper class
C. hurt the expansion of the nation-state concept
D. encouraged effective governmental bureaucracy

Ans: D
Diff: H
Page: 523

3. According to Thomas Hobbes:
A. the state of nature once actually existed
B. the state of nature was not pleasant
C. people have the right to make a social contract, and to break a social contract
D. majority rule of property owners is the ideal form of government

Ans: B
Diff: M
Page: 524

4. John Locke argued that:
A. people had been forced into the social contract
B. people had a right to replace a government that broke the social contract
C. divine-right monarchy was the best form of government
D. individuals found freedom when they acquiesced to the general will of the populace

Ans: B
Diff: E
Page: 524

5. Which of the following scholars pioneered the notion that the sun was at the center of the solar system?
A. Nicholas Copernicus
B. Galileo Galilei
C. Tycho Brahe
D. Isaac Newton

Ans: A
Diff: M
Page: 528

6. T F John Locke had a more positive view of the state of nature than did Thomas Hobbes.

Ans: T
Diff: M
Page: 524

7. T F Galileo forced the Catholic Church to admit that his view of the heliocentric model of the solar system was correct.

Ans: F
Diff: E
Page: 529

8. T F Unfortunately, the scientific discoveries of the eighteenth century produced few, if any, practical applications.

Ans: F
Diff: M
Page: 530

9. Define the term revolution, and then discuss the shared outcomes of the three major revolutions that occurred between 1688 and 1789.

Diff: H
Pages: 523-524

10. Describe the views of John Locke on the following: the state of nature, the social contract, the right of revolution, who should govern, property rights.

Diff: M
Pages: 524-525

11. Which of the following occurred before the Glorious Revolution?
A. the French Revolution
B. the English monarchy was restored
C. Galileo's death
D. John Locke wrote the *Second Treatise on Government*

Ans: C
Diff: E
Page: 522

12. Charles I of England:
A. had to deal with a budget surplus by the late 1630s
B. wanted to call Parliament into session
C. refused to grant Parliament's demand for an elected legislature
D. converted to Catholicism

Ans: C
Diff: E
Page: 531

13. The Bill of Rights created through the Glorious Revolution:
A. provided for parliamentary approval of tax increases
B. provided for religious freedom
C. specifically excluded the American colonies from its provisions
D. was opposed by William of Orange

Ans: A
Diff: M
Page: 532

14. Many *philosophes* were deists, which meant that they felt:
A. the world was populated by many gods and goddesses
B. the government should support the Roman Catholic church
C. there had been a creator of the world, but it was no longer a significant presence
D. there should be no separation of church and state

Ans: C
Diff: H
Page: 533

15. The *Encyclopedia*:
A. in general argued against revolutionary change
B. had little impact on the Enlightenment
C. was written in large part by Jean-Jacques Rousseau
D. presented important ideas of the *philosophes*

Ans: D
Diff: M
Page: 534

16. Of the following, who was NOT an enlightened despot?
A. James II of England
B. Frederick II of Prussia
C. Catherine the Great of Russia
D. Joseph II of Austria

Ans: A
Diff: E
Page: 535

17. T F Oliver Cromwell led Parliament in the removal and execution of Charles I.

Ans: T
Diff: E
Page: 531

18. T F Montesquieu's ideas on separation of powers within government had an influence on the writers of the American constitution.

Ans: T
Diff: M
Page: 533

19. T F Voltaire argued that enlightened despotism was preferable to badly administered self-rule.

Ans: T
Diff: E
Page: 535

20. The ideas of the Enlightenment had a profound impact on the world. Discuss and analyze the major concepts developed and propagated by the major thinkers of the Enlightenment.

Diff: M
Pages: 533-536

21. Both Voltaire and Rousseau were skeptical of democratic government. What did they advocate instead? Why?

Diff: H
Page: 535

22. E.P. Thompson recounts a discussion between General Ireton and common soldiers concerning universal suffrage. Contrast the two positions and explain which you find the most convincing.

Diff: M
Page: 532

23. The most fundamental reason for the American Revolution was that:
A. American colonists felt they were not being given their full rights as Englishmen
B. American colonists did not want to pay higher taxes
C. American colonists resented the presence of so many British troops in the colonies
D. American colonists wanted the freedom to expand westward across the continent

Ans: A
Diff: H
Page: 536

24. The American Bill of Rights provided for all of the following, except:
A. freedom of religion
B. the right to vote
C. the right to assemble
D. the right to bear arms

Ans: B
Diff: M
Page: 537

25. The 1789 Estates General:
A. was under the control of Louis XVI
B. was called to meet by the first estate
C. had no representation for the lower classes of France
D. had its most radical representatives in the third estate

Ans: D
Diff: M
Page: 540

26. In 1789, the National Assembly:
A. was dominated by the aristocracy and clergy
B. issued the "Declaration of the Rights of Man and the Citizen"
C. decided to maintain serfdom
D. preserved the tithe for the Catholic church

Ans: B
Diff: E
Page: 541

27. The Committee on Public Safety:
A. was formed by the *Girondins*
B. abolished the national draft
C. executed Robespierre as one of its first orders of business
D. instituted the Reign of Terror

Ans: D
Diff: M
Page: 543

28. Napoleon:
A. was more oppressive than any of the so-called enlightened despots
B. was a traitor to everything the French Revolution stood for
C. sought to export French political and social ideas to other European countries
D. conquered Russia early in his reign

Ans: C
Diff: M
Page: 546

29. T F The large number of religious dissenters in the American colonies made the revolution there easier to accomplish.

Ans: T
Diff: M
Page: 537

30. T F During its first two years, the French Revolution was similar in result to the American Revolution.

Ans: T
Diff: H
Page: 542

31. T F French armies under Napoleon oppressed Jews throughout Europe.

Ans: F
Diff: M
Page: 545

32. First describe the grievances the American colonists had against the King of England. Then discuss important provisions in the American Bill of Rights.

Diff: M
Page: 537

33. Discuss the following aspects of the French Revolution: the reasons why it started, the composition of the Estates General, the accomplishments of the revolution through its first two years.

Diff: H
Pages: 540-542

34. Napoleon was one of the most influential people in the history of Europe. Write an essay that discusses how he came to power, his important domestic policies, the policies he implemented in the territories he controlled outside of France, and why he eventually fell from power.

Diff: H
Pages: 545-547

35. Which of the following American territories was gained through warfare?
A. Louisiana Territory
B. Gadsden Purchase
C. Utah Territory
D. Texas

Ans: C
Diff: M
Page: 539

36. T F For expressing both royalism and feminism, Marie Gouges was guillotined by the radical Jacobins in 1793.

Ans: T
Diff: E
Page: 543

37. Identify and explain the three interpretive perspectives concerning the French Revolution. Explain which you find to be the most convincing.

Diff: M
Page: 544

38. Of the following territories, which was never under Napoleon's control?
A. Italy
B. Spain
C. Britain
D. Netherlands

Ans: C
Diff: E
Page: 546

39. Which school of thought on the abolition of the slave trade argued that slavery violated human nature?
A. *philosophes*
B. economic critique
C. compassion
D. fear of revolt

Ans: A
Diff: M
Page: 549

40. The slave revolution in Saint-Domingue:
A. began as a response to the French Revolution
B. occurred despite the fact that slaves made up less than one-third of the population
C. was eventually suppressed by Napoleon
D. was sparked by a man who eventually died in France

Ans: D
Diff: M
Page: 548

41. The Saint-Domingue revolt
A. ended in defeat for the Haitian slaves
B. fractured the hope for unity among black and mulatto armies
C. was the only known successful slave revolution in history
D. led to more oppressive treatment of slaves

Ans: C
Diff: M
Page: 548

42. Of the following countries, which was the first to abolish slavery?
A. Britain
B. United States
C. Brazil
D. Cuba

Ans: A
Diff: E
Page: 550

43. Despite the abolition of slavery in the United States in 1865, the Atlantic slave trade continued until it was abolished in Brazil in:
A. 1888
B. 1950
C. 1914
D. 1927

Ans: A
Diff: M
Page: 550

44. T F Maroons were persons of mixed race, usually with European and African parents.

Ans: F
Diff: M
Page: 547

45. T F The slave revolt in Haiti is the only known successful slave revolt in history.

Ans: T
Diff: M
Page: 548

46. T F Brazil's bid for independence led to a long and bloody war with Portugal.

Ans: F
Diff: E
Pages: 553-554

47. Explain why the slave revolt at Saint-Domingue was the only slave revolution in history to succeed.

Diff: M
Page: 548

48. The British abolished the slave trade in 1807 and in 1833 they abolished slavery throughout the empire. The United States followed their lead, abolishing the slave trade in 1808 and abolishing slavery in 1865. Explain why the trade did not effectively end until 1888.

Diff: M
Page: 550

49. T F Haiti was granted its independence from France in 1804.

Ans: T
Diff: E
Page: 547

50. Compare the four different schools of thought regarding the principle reason for the abolition of slavery. In your opinion, which school has the most merit? Support your conclusion.

Diff: H
Page: 549

51. The early-nineteenth-century Latin American revolutions:
A. did not begin until the late 1820s
B. were led primarily by creole elites
C. were usually even more radical than the French Revolution
D. did not draw inspiration from either the American or the French revolutions

Ans: B
Diff: M
Page: 550

52. Which of the following groups gained the most in the Latin American revolutions?
A. mestizos
B. Amerindians
C. creole elites
D. Europeans

Ans: C
Diff: E
Page: 551

53. In the first half of the nineteenth century, Mexico:
A. was ruled by a monarch for all but two years
B. increased the size of its territorial holdings
C. was helped in its independence movement by two Catholic priests
D. had a stable government

Ans: C
Diff: M
Page: 553

54. Many new nations of Latin America sought to increase their power by:
A. waging war against their neighbors
B. confiscating Church lands
C. industrializing their economy
D. creating their own empires

Ans: B
Diff: M
Page: 555

55. In *A Tale of Two Cities*, Charles Dickens depicts the revolution in
A. England
B. the American colonies
C. Brazil
D. France

Ans: D
Diff: E
Page: 556

56. T F Tupac Amaru led an unsuccessful revolt against Spanish rule in Peru in 1780.

Ans: T
Diff: E
Page: 550

57. T F After gaining independence, most Latin American nations moved to strengthen the power of the Catholic Church.

Ans: F
Diff: E
Page: 555

58. T F The new nations throughout Latin America soon became economically dependent on their former colonizers.

Ans: T
Diff: E
Page: 557

59. Describe the unique features of Paraguay's development between independence and the mid-1860s. What put a stop to this development?

Diff: M
Page: 554

60. Contrast the positive results of the French revolution with its negative repercussions. Was this pattern repeated in any of the other revolutions of the period? Explain.

Diff: M
Page: 557

61. Which South American country was the last to obtain its independence?
A. United Provinces of Central America
B. New Granada
C. Peru
D. Mexico

Ans: B
Diff: M
Page: 551

62. The most recent transfer of territory from Mexico to the United States was:
A. Texas
B. California
C. New Mexico
D. the Gadsden Purchase

Ans: D
Diff: M
Page: 553

63. Explain how Chilean writer Pablo Neruda envisioned Latin America in *Canto General*. Who does he blame for this situation, and why?

Diff: M
Page: 555

1. The industrial revolution resulted in all of the following outcomes, except:
A. a lower aggregate standard of living
B. changes in where people worked
C. a different pattern of relations among countries
D. different methods of fighting wars

Ans: A
Diff: E
Page: 563

2. The industrial revolution began in:
A. the United States
B. Britain
C. France
D. Germany

Ans: B
Diff: E
Page: 563

3. British workers engaged in the putting-out system in the textile industry:
A. usually made better wages than workers in textile factories
B. were more likely to keep their jobs in a recession than were textile-factory workers
C. occasionally engaged in Luddite riots
D. were the mainstay of the British textile industry well into the twentieth century

Ans: C
Diff: M
Page: 567

4. Which of the following was NOT a result of the invention of the cotton gin?
A. dramatic increase in American cotton production
B. improvement in the working conditions for slaves
C. expansion of plantation agriculture into new territories
D. increased demand for slaves

Ans: B
Diff: M
Page: 567

5. As a result of transatlantic steamship lines, the world steamship tonnage increased:
A. more than 100 times
B. nearly 50 times
C. more than 10 times
D. nearly 500 times

Ans: A
Diff: E
Page: 569

6. T F Enclosure laws in England between 1714 and 1801 resulted in one-fourth of the land in Britain being converted from community property to private property.

Ans: T
Diff: E
Pages: 563-564

7. T F In the middle of the eighteenth century, woolens replaced cotton as the most commonly used textile in Britain.

Ans: F
Diff: E
Page: 565

8. T F The new canal systems quickly superseded the steam-powered locomotives.

Ans: F
Diff: E
Page: 568

9. Explain the development of the agricultural revolution and clarify its role in the development of the industrial revolution.

Diff: M
Page: 563

10. Write an essay in which you discuss the development and application of iron, steam, engines, railways, and steam ships.

Diff: M
Pages: 567-569

11. Which of the following innovations was the most recently developed?
A. machine gun
B. typewriter
C. cotton gin
D. telegraph

Ans: B
Diff: E
Page: 562

12. T F Railway development was significantly more prevalent in Great Britain than in France by 1850.

Ans: T
Diff: M
Page: 566

13. Of the following technological innovations, which was developed first?
A. the cotton gin
B. the steam ship
C. the steam locomotive
D. the spinning jenny

Ans: D
Diff: E
Page: 568

14. Britain was the birthplace of the industrial revolution. What were the major innovations of the revolution there between 1740 and 1860?

Diff: M
Pages: 565-569

15. Compare Wordsworth's impression of London with that of Blake. Explain why they reach different conclusions.

Diff: M
Page: 570

16. In the late nineteenth century, the chemical industry:
A. relied primarily on plants as sources of chemicals
B. stressed the importance of the use of alkalis
C. had yet to produce artificial fertilizers
D. created chemical explosives

Ans: D
Diff: M
Page: 571

17. Thomas Edison's most important single act was the:
A. formation of a private industrial development lab
B. invention of the telegraph
C. invention of the kinetoscope
D. invention the light bulb

Ans: A
Diff: H
Page: 572

18. Factory production in the late nineteenth century was characterized by:
A. numerous small- to medium-sized firms in any given industry
B. displacement of artisans in many industries
C. a forty-hour work week
D. a concern for worker safety

Ans: B
Diff: E
Page: 572

19. Which of the following statements about the industrial revolution is NOT true?
A. Toward its end, death rates fell
B. Population increased as industrialization progressed
C. It was often accompanied by the formation of cartels
D. Toward its end, family size increased

Ans: D
Diff: M
Page: 575

20. Who benefited the most from the industrial revolution?
A. factory owners
B. artisans
C. miners
D. factory workers

Ans: A
Diff: M
Page: 575

21. T F The second stage of the industrial revolution saw steel produced cheaply.

Ans: T
Diff: E
Page: 571

22. France was the largest foreign investor in industry in the Americas in the nineteenth century.

Ans: F
Diff: M
Page: 573

23. T F Parents of the working class often tried to get around regulations restricting child labor.

Ans: T
Diff: M
Page: 576

24. Describe the impact of industrialization on working class family life. How did industrialization affect the relationship between men and women?

Diff: M
Pages: 574-577

25. Describe how the new standard of "domesticity" affected the status of working class and immigrant women.

Diff: M
Pages: 577-578

26. Which of the following innovations was developed first?
A. telephone
B. Gatling gun
C. refrigerator
D. motorcycle

Ans: C
Diff: E
Page: 573

27. A demonstration at St. Peter's Fields in Manchester in 1819:
A. quickly led to mob rioting
B. was met with violence by the military
C. called for an increase on the tariff on grain
D. was the first time the Chartists presented their petition to Parliament

Ans: B
Diff: M
Page: 579

28. The British Parliament did all of the following in the nineteenth century, except:
A. provide for universal male suffrage
B. repeal the Corn Laws
C. pass Poor Laws
D. legalize labor unions

Ans: A
Diff: E
Page: 579

29. Labor organizing in Britain:
A. began in the mid 1830s, according to historian E.P. Thompson
B. initially had its greatest success among unskilled workers
C. was legalized in the 1870s
D. was discouraged by the Fabian Society

Ans: C
Diff: M
Page: 581

30. Marx believed that wealth was produced primarily by:
A. financiers
B. capitalists
C. workers
D. the government

Ans: C
Diff: E
Page: 583

31. This was the first European country to have a political party based on working-class support:
A. France
B. Britain
C. Germany
D. Spain

Ans: C
Diff: E
Page: 584

32. America's most successful nineteenth-century labor union was the:
A. Industrial Workers of the World
B. Knights of Labor
C. Congress of Industrial Organizations
D. American Federation of Labor

Ans: D
Diff: M
Page: 584

33. T F Shortly after the Peterloo Massacre, the Corn Laws were abolished.

Ans: F
Diff: M
Page: 579

34. T F Karl Marx thought the struggle between classes was what moved history forward.

Ans: T
Diff: H
Page: 583

35. T F Because of the way the Paris Commune ended, the French labor movement lost many of its leaders.

Ans: T
Diff: E
Page: 586

36. Describe and analyze the thought of Karl Marx on the following subjects: the production of wealth, the nature of the capitalist system, the necessity of revolution, the primary force in history, the importance of economics to human relationships. Was there any truth to the perspectives of Marx? Did he bring any lasting insight into human actions or the human condition?

Diff: H
Pages: 582-584

37. Describe the impact of industrialization on workers in China and India. Explain the benefits and drawbacks of indentured servitude upon these populations.

Diff: M
Page: 586-588

38. Of the following milestones in women's emancipation, which occurred the most recently?
A. banning of ritual suicide by Hindu widows
B. the beginning of the end of footbinding in China
C. the feminist writings of Mary Wollstonecraft
D. Seneca Falls convention

Ans: B
Diff: M
Page: 582

39. Describe the position of Pandita Ramabai concerning the impact of foreign goods on India. What was she proposing and why?

Diff: M
Page: 587

40. This was the greatest contributor to urban growth in the nineteenth century:
A. government policies promoting city growth
B. industrialization
C. nationalism
D. a decline in agricultural output

Ans: B
Diff: M
Page: 588

41. According to Max Weber, the new industrial cities were
A. worse than medieval cities
B. a vast improvement over medieval cities
C. an indication of positive future
D. creating stronger, more stable social institutions

Ans: A
Diff: M
Page: 589

42. Oswald Spengler:
A. founded the discipline of sociology
B. felt that the division of labor common in urban factories helped create a sense of individuality in workers
C. had an optimistic view of cities
D. thought cities destroyed the spirit of the people who created them

Ans: D
Diff: M
Page: 590

43. English businessman Charles Booth:
A. helped produce a slim book on the conditions of the working class in Manchester, England
B. wanted to know how he could squeeze more work out of his employees
C. wanted to understand the problems of urban poverty in order to combat them
D. avoided the political ramifications of his studies

Ans: C
Diff: M
Page: 590

44. Of the following people, who was most optimistic about the social conditions prevailing in late-nineteenth-century cities?
A. Adna Ferrin Weber
B. Karl Marx
C. Vladimir Lenin
D. Friedrich Engels

Ans: A
Diff: E
Page: 591

45. In its study of Chicago, the "Chicago school of urban ecology" found that:
A. most people lived in the downtown area
B. the city's many neighborhoods provided a sense of community
C. as a city's population increased, its diversity decreased
D. city life killed the spirit and led to a lost sense of self

Ans: B
Diff: M
Page: 592

46. When confronted with the various problems of urban crowding, British reformer Ebenezer Howard proposed:
A. building skyscrapers
B. building small towns in rural areas
C. having a core city surrounded by suburbs and greenbelts
D. initiating massive government spending for social welfare programs and pollution control

Ans: C
Diff: M
Page: 593

47. T F There is no connection between industrialization and urbanization.

Ans: F
Diff: E
Page: 588

48. T F Innovations in transportation led to the development of commercial, cultural, industrial and residential districts within cities.

Ans: T
Diff: E
Page: 592

49. T F Almost ten million people found employment as indentured servants during the industrial revolution.

Ans: T
Diff: E
Page: 593

50. Describe and analyze the factors that need to be considered when evaluating urban life during the late nineteenth century. Does the analysis produce conclusions that are more positive or more negative?

Diff: H
Page: 592

51. How did the garden city concept seek to transform urban planning?

Diff: E
Page: 593

52. T F Walt Whitman had a pessimistic view of the cities of nineteenth-century America.

Ans: F
Diff: M
Page: 588

53. Compare Adna Ferrin Weber's examination of urban life to that of Marx and Engels. What do you think shaped Weber's more positive assessment?

Diff: M
Page: 591

54. Adna Ferrin Weber, who studied nineteenth-century urbanization:
A. received his Ph.D. from Cambridge University
B. focused his study on England
C. used statistical analysis to help formulate his conclusions
D. relied primarily on in-depth case studies of individual immigrants to cities

Ans: C
Diff: M
Page: 591

1. *The Declaration of the Rights of Man and Citizen*:
A. proclaimed allegiance to an ethnic group
B. specifically renounced the formation of a social contract
C. called for attachment to the French nation
D. had little impact on the French people

Ans: C
Diff: H
Page: 597

2. Nationalism was first a major force in:
A. Japan
B. Germany
C. France
D. Italy

Ans: C
Diff: H
Page: 598

3. American nationalism was initially forged by:
A. the political will of its early leaders
B. the bonds of history stretching back to pre-evolutionary times
C. the shared faith of Christianity
D. a belief in the benefits of capitalism

Ans: A
Diff: M
Page: 600

4. In Europe in the early and middle decades of the nineteenth century:
A. the Congress of Vienna had little success in achieving its goals regarding nationalism
B. Italy won independence in 1848
C. Belgium remained a part of Holland
D. cultural nationalism was growing in Germany

Ans: D
Diff: M
Page: 603

5. Zionism in Europe:
A. became a significant force in the middle of the eighteenth century
B. was based on Jewish nationalism
C. was never fulfilled
D. was opposed by Theodor Herzl

Ans: B
Diff: E
Page: 604

6. T F Upper and Lower Canada shared the same language and history.

Ans: F
Diff: H
Page: 599

7. T F Irish nationalism surged in the wake of the Act of Union in 1801 that threatened to annihilate the Gaelic language.

Ans: T
Diff: M
Page: 600

8. T F Zionism led many Jews to establish a colony in Palestine.

Ans: T
Diff: E
Page: 604

9. How did nationalism lead to the creation of Germany?

Diff: M
Page: 603

10. Describe Zionism, including its roots and goals.

Diff: E
Page: 605

11. Which rebellion occurred first?
A. Maji-Maji revolt
B. Taiping Rebellion
C. First War for National Independence
D. Boxer Rebellion

Ans: B
Diff: E
Page: 598

12. T F By 1871, the German Empire included the Alsace and Lorraine regions.

Ans: T
Diff: E
Page: 601

13. T F The Papal States were annexed by Italy in 1860.

Ans: F
Diff: E
Page: 601

14. Compare the definitions of nationalism presented by Joseph-Ernest Renan and Benedict Anderson. What common themes can you identify in their positions?

Diff: M
Page: 603

15. In the second half of the nineteenth century, India:
A. exported large quantities of cotton textiles to Britain
B. exported machined goods to much of Europe
C. had no significant transportation system linking the major regions of the country
D. was ruled directly by the British

Ans: D
Diff: M
Pages: 604, 612

16. In the nineteenth century, the Ottoman Empire:
A. lost control of Anatolia
B. ruled its subjects through their religious communities
C. won a major victory in the Crimean War
D. undertook a successful industrialization program

Ans: B
Diff: M
Page: 608

17. The industrial revolution in Britain ruined this, India's largest domestic industry.
A. leather production
B. tea production
C. cotton textile production
D. jute production

Ans: C
Diff: M
Page: 611

18. The Opium Wars:
A. took place in the early twentieth century
B. were fought primarily by France and China
C. resulted in a substantial loss of sovereignty for China
D. quickly shut down the flow of opium into China

Ans: C
Diff: M
Page: 616

19. The Boxer Rebellion:
A. was begun by a group of nationalists
B. ended with the acquisition of power by Sun Yat-sen
C. resulted in direct British control of China
D. was crushed by a combination of imperial powers

Ans: D
Diff: M
Page: 617

20. T F In 1857, India successfully defeated Britain in the "First War for National Independence."

Ans: F
Diff: E
Page: 612

21. T F The Taiping Rebellion resulted in the deaths of about 20 million people.

Ans: T
Diff: E
Page: 616

22. T F By the end of the nineteenth century, France was the dominant power in Indochina.

Ans: T
Diff: E
Page: 609

23. In the nineteenth century the Ottoman Empire was referred to as the "Sick Man of Europe." What happened to its empire, both internally and externally during this time period?

Diff: M
Pages: 608-609

24. Describe the major events--domestic and involving other countries--that showed the weakness of the Manchu dynasty in China from 1800 to 1914.

Diff: H
Page: 616

25. Which continent witnessed the greatest number of anti-colonial revolts between 1815 and 1870?
A. North America
B. South America
C. Asia
D. Africa

Ans: B
Diff: M
Page: 605

26. Which European nation controlled the largest geographic area in Africa?
A. Italy
B. Germany
C. France
D. Belgium

Ans: C
Diff: M
Page: 606

27. T F When Britain founded the city of Singapore, they divided the city into separate districts for the various ethnic groups that resided there.

Ans: T
Diff: E
Page: 610

28. Explain the future of India as envisioned by the poet Dalpatram Kavi.

Diff: M
Page: 612

29. Which foreign power made the most extensive inroads into southern China?
A. France
B. Britain
C. Germany
D. Japan

Ans: A
Diff: M
Page: 615

30. In sub-Saharan Africa, European control was limited to
A. the shoreline of the east coast
B. the Congo region
C. the shoreline of the west coast
D. the Sudan

Ans: C
Diff: E
Page: 618

31. Which of the following movements did NOT help create the *mfecane* in southern and eastern Africa?
A. Boer Trek
B. the migration of refugees displaced by the Boers and Zulus
C. Shaka's Zulu expansion
D. British Army

Ans: D
Diff: M
Page: 620

32. Between 1798 and 1881, Egypt:
A. was firmly under the control of the Ottoman Empire
B. sought to seize territory from the Ottoman Empire
C. refused to have relations with Britain
D. was controlled by France

Ans: B
Diff: M
Page: 621

33. Henry Morton Stanley:
A. precipitated the Fashoda crisis between France and Britain
B. worked as an agent of King Leopold II of Belgium
C. never did find Dr. Livingstone
D. was motivated primarily by the desire to spread Christianity

Ans: B
Diff: M
Page: 627

34. The 1884-85 Berlin conference on Africa:
A. gave the Congo to Holland
B. prohibited settlement of the internal portion of Africa
C. apportioned adjoining territory of a given European colony to that colony's European country
D. ended in a colonial war involving most of the major European powers

Ans: C
Diff: M
Page: 627

35. T F South Africa passed from Dutch hands to British hands after the Napoleonic wars.

Ans: T
Diff: M
Page: 618

36. T F It took the British three years to defeat the Boers in South Africa.

Ans: T
Diff: E
Page: 620

37. T F The French lost their battle against the army of al-Qadir in 1871.

Ans: F
Diff: M
Page: 622

38. Describe the efforts of the United States to establish the colony of Liberia. Evaluate the success of this endeavor.

Diff: M
Page: 624

39. Explain the impact of European land ownership upon the labor of Africans. What were the alternative forms of employment? Did this resolve the labor issues; why or why not?

Diff: M
Page: 628

40. Which European nation was the most active in West Africa during the late nineteenth century?
A. Britain
B. France
C. Portugal
D. Germany

Ans: B
Diff: E
Page: 619

41. The text presents several different historical interpretations of European colonialism. Describe and analyze three of these, and then give your own supported conclusion.

Diff: H
Page: 626

42. Which of the following was NOT a common role for local women in a colonial society?
A. sexual partner
B. cultural negotiator
C. translator
D. wife

Ans: D
Diff: M
Page: 629

43. Armed revolts and nonviolent political movements against colonial rule encompassed which of the following in their new governments?
A. the repudiation of all innovations introduced by colonial powers
B. the incorporation of pre-colonial institutions as well as new ones introduced by colonial powers
C. the repudiation of all pre-colonial institutions
D. the creation of a system with no connection to either the pre-colonial or colonial past

Ans: B
Diff: M
Page: 631

44. In 1867, Japan was unified by all of the following aspects, except:
A. an integrated national political structure
B. use of a common language
C. a single dynasty of emperors
D. agreement of purpose among the leaders of the *hans*

Ans: D
Diff: M
Page: 632

45. The end of the shogunate in 1868 was precipitated by all of the following, except:
A. an uprising of peasants
B. dissatisfied young samurai
C. the earlier actions of Commodore Matthew Perry
D. foreign actions on Japanese soil

Ans: A
Diff: M
Pages: 632-633

46. The main purpose of the Meiji Restoration was to:
A. distribute land from large holders to peasants
B. strengthen the economy and the military
C. ensure that women received the same rights as men
D. remove power from the emperor

Ans: B
Diff: E
Pages: 634-635

47. The Meiji government:
A. refused to undertake public works projects
B. moved the capital from Tokyo to the island of Kyoto
C. took the land of the *daimyo*
D. refused to subsidize important samurai

Ans: C
Diff: M
Page: 634

48. In the latter part of the nineteenth century, Japan:
A. forced foreigners to leave the country
B. abolished worship of the emperor
C. promoted the welfare of peasants over that of their landlords
D. undertook large-scale industrialization

Ans: D
Diff: M
Page: 635

49. T F In colonial areas, European women generally sought to keep European men from having sex with local women.

Ans: T
Diff: E
Page: 629

50. T F The Budi Utomo was the first nationalist association of Indonesia.

Ans: T
Diff: E
Page: 631

51. T F After the Meiji Restoration, Japan eagerly sought contact with the West.

Ans: T
Diff: E
Page: 636

52. T F The Meiji Restoration led the way for women to achieve legal equality with men within three decades.

Ans: F
Diff: E
Page: 638

53. First discuss the qualities of the shogunate that led to the Meiji restoration. Then present the important policies of the Meiji government, including restructuring efforts in government itself and in the economy.

Diff: H
Pages: 631-635

54. In an essay, describe and analyze Japanese actions to become a colonial power and gain military equivalence with the major European nations in the last part of the nineteenth century and the early part of the twentieth century. How effective was Japan in achieving these goals?

Diff: M
Pages: 631-639

55. T F By 1872, Japan had an educational plan to provide teaching to 90 per cent of Japanese children by 1900.

Ans: T
Diff: E
Page: 633

56. Describe Fukuzawa Yukichi's interpretation of the West. What do his observations reveal about the cultural differences between Japan and the West?

Diff: M
Page: 634

57. Which of the following was NOT controlled by Japan by 1900?
A. Korea
B. Kurile Islands
C. Shandong
D. Taiwan

Ans: A
Diff: M
Page: 637

58. T F Russia evacuated Manchuria and recognized Japanese interests in Korea as a result of the peace agreement mediated by Theodore Roosevelt.

Ans: T
Diff: E
Page: 639

1. Which of the following did NOT contribute to shattered illusions about the future?
A. World War I
B. global economic depression
C. improved standards of living
D. World War II

Ans: C
Diff: E
Page: 646

2. In the second half of the twentieth century, which of the following encouraged optimism?
A. conflicts over gender identity
B. ethnic and religious violence
C. unequal distribution of wealth
D. advancements in communication technology

Ans: D
Diff: M
Page: 647

3. T F In the first half of the twentieth century many naively overemphasized the positive impact of technology.

Ans: T
Diff: E
Page: 646

4. T F Technologies of destruction brought an end to any positive benefits from technology.

Ans: F
Diff: M
Page: 647

5. Examine two major benefits from technological innovation and two ways in which it impeded or imperiled the global population.

Diff: M
Pages: 646-647

6. The United Nations' first World Conference on women's issues took place in which of the following?
A. Cairo
B. Mexico City
C. Copenhagen
D. Beijing

Ans: B
Diff: E
Page: 802

7. Which of the following is NOT one of the major environmental concerns that provoked international action?
A. global warming
B. the production of toxic chemicals and gases
C. deforestation of the rainforest
D. global poverty

Ans: D
Diff: M
Page: 802

8. T F The United States embraced the Kyoto Agreement as a necessary step toward protecting the environment.

Ans: F
Diff: M
Page: 802

9. T F According to President Bush, Islamic militancy poses the greatest current threat to the United States.

Ans: T
Diff: E
Page: 803

10. Compare the status of women in post-industrial nations with that of women in developing nations. Identify and explain the key areas of difference.

Diff: M
Pages: 802-803

1. Internal combustion engines were first used in automobiles in which of the following:
A. the United States
B. France
C. Germany
D. Switzerland

Ans: C
Diff: E
Page: 651

2. Einstein argued that:
A. light possessed only a wave-like nature
B. neither time nor motion is fixed
C. the speed of light varies over time
D. mass and energy are not interchangeable

Ans: B
Diff: M
Page: 652

3. Sigmund Freud thought that the prime motivation for humanity was:
A. reason
B. love
C. fear
D. sex

Ans: D
Diff: M
Page: 653

4. Which of the following people pioneered birth control in the United States?
A. Marie Stopes
B. Theodore Van Velde
C. Margaret Sanger
D. Karen Horney

Ans: C
Diff: E
Page: 653

5. From 1880 to 1913, which nation experienced the greatest gain in manufacturing productivity?
A. Germany
B. United States
C. Britain
D. France

Ans: B
Diff: E
Page: 654

6. T F In 1913, Henry Ford's assembly-line production built one car every 93 minutes

Ans: T
Diff: E
Page: 651

7. T F By 1910, the average life expectancy in the United States reached 68 years.

Ans: F
Diff: E
Page: 651

8. T F Despite the build-up of armed forces, the balance of power between the Triple Alliance and Triple Entente was expected to deter war.

Ans: T
Diff: M
Page: 654

9. List eight examples of the way technology has affected humans.

Diff: E
Page: 649

10. Describe how technology affected sexuality and gender relationships in industrialized nations.

Diff: M
Page: 653

11. Which of the following was NOT an area of British rule protested by the Indians?
A. economic and technological policies
B. political policies
C. social welfare programs
D. religious policies

Ans: C
Diff: M
Page: 656

12. The 1911 revolution in China:
A. ended with Sun Yat-sen in power
B. was suppressed, with the emperor ruling for another 25 years
C. quickly led to the end of the Manchu dynasty
D. brought the rule of the warlords to an end

Ans: C
Diff: M
Page: 656

13. This was NOT one of Sun Yat-sen's "three principles":
A. Marxist economics
B. state-owned enterprises
C. democracy
D. nationalism

Ans: A
Diff: M
Page: 657

14. In Mexico during the leadership of Porfirio Díaz:
A. the salaries of urban workers increased
B. the lives of peasants improved
C. exports of agricultural products increased
D. nearly one-half of all peasants lived on land they owned

Ans: C
Diff: M
Page: 659

15. Emiliano Zapata:
A. eventually became president of Mexico
B. was one of the more conservative Mexican revolutionaries
C. fought several battles with Pancho Villa
D. was a favorite of the peasants

Ans: D
Diff: M
Page: 659

16. Obregón:
A. excluded labor from his government
B. formed the Party of Revolutionary Institutions
C. allowed indigenous Indians a place in government
D. nationalized foreign-owned oil companies

Ans: C
Diff: M
Page: 661

17. T F The increasing pace of scientific development and technological application intensified the displacement of traditional ways of production, especially in regions formerly under colonial rule.

Ans: T
Diff: E
Page: 655

18. T F Sun Yat-sen argued that China's economic problem was lack of production rather than unequal distribution.

Ans: T
Diff: E
Page: 658

19. T F In 1910, Mexico was one of the less economically advanced countries in Latin America.

Ans: F
Diff: M
Page: 659

20. T F Diego Rivera often chose themes from Mexico's history for his art work.

Ans: T
Diff: E
Page: 660

21. Identify and explain Sun Yat-sen's "Three People's Principles." In what ways did he adopt western philosophies and policies in the program?

Diff: M
Pages: 657-658

22. What were the important reforms proposed by Mexican revolutionary Emiliano Zapata?

Diff: E
Pages: 659-660

23. Which of the following did NOT help bring about the end of the Ottoman Empire?

A. an Arab revolt
B. Internal dissent
C. Turkish defeat in World War I
D. a British invasion

Ans: D
Diff: M
Page: 662

24. T F Kuwait became a British protectorate in 1914.

Ans: T
Diff: M
Page: 662

25. World War I:
A. began when Germany invaded Belgium
B. had its roots in the Serbian government's desire to seize Austrian territory
C. saw the first use of the machine gun in battle
D. involved more countries world-wide than World War II did

Ans: A
Diff: M
Page: 663

26. This country fought on the side of Great Britain in World War I:
A. Ottoman Empire
B. Austria-Hungary
C. Italy
D. Bulgaria

Ans: C
Diff: E
Page: 663

27. American involvement in World War I:
A. was certain from the first day of the war
B. began with an American declaration of war in 1915
C. had the support of nearly the entire populace
D. was decisive in defeating Germany and its allies

Ans: D
Diff: M
Page: 666

28. This was NOT one of the provisions of the Treaty of Versailles:
A. immediate independence for colonies
B. payment of reparations by Germany
C. creation of new states in Central Europe
D. dissolution of the Ottoman Empire

Ans: A
Diff: E
Page: 670

29. The League of Nations:
A. had several early successes
B. was essentially a tool of the United States, since it was the most powerful member
C. refused to end European colonialism
D. forced Italy to withdraw its military from Ethiopia

Ans: C
Diff: M
Pages: 670-671

30. T F By the end of World War I, approximately 8.5 million soldiers had died.

Ans: T
Diff: E
Page: 665

31. T F The Zimmermann telegram persuaded Mexico to join with Germany against the United States.

Ans: F
Diff: M
Page: 666

32. T F The League of Nations had little enforcement power for the decisions it made.

Ans: T
Diff: E
Page: 672

33. Explain how the European alliance system contributed to the escalation of war following the assassination of Archduke Franz Ferdinand and his wife in 1914.

Diff: M
Page: 663

34. What were the major provisions of the Versailles Treaty? Do you think Germany was treated fairly? Did the treaty make World War II more or less likely? Support your answer.

Diff: H
Page: 670

35. Which of the following was NOT a member of the Central Powers?
A. Bulgaria
B. Austria-Hungary
C. Italy
D. Germany

Ans: C
Diff: E
Page: 664

36. What does Indian journalist Idulal Yagnik write about the relationship between European soldiers and the people they colonized? Why do you think the white soldiers believed the local women possessed an "independent temper"?

Diff: M
Page: 666

37. Which of the following became the first state to gain its independence at the end of World War I?
A. Saudi Arabia
B. Poland
C. Ukraine
D. Iraq

Ans: B
Diff: M
Page: 668

38. Czar Alexander II:
A. freed the serfs
B. tightened press censorship
C. did little to industrialize Russia
D. took power after Russia's defeat in the Crimean War

Ans: A
Diff: M
Page: 673

39. Prior to the Bolshevik Revolution, Russia's agriculture had all of the following characteristics, except:
A. the government allowed unregulated buying and selling of agricultural land
B. the peasantry lived in collective villages (*mirs*)
C. productivity was stagnant
D. a strong class distinction existed between peasants and large landowners

Ans: A
Diff: M
Page: 673

40. In Russia in 1905, all of the following happened, except:
A. loss of a war with Japan
B. "Bloody Sunday"
C. creation of a *duma*
D. the abdication of the czar

Ans: D
Diff: E
Page: 674

41. Lenin's New Economic Policy:
A. was a more Marxist approach to the economy than his 1918-20 policy
B. put even more restrictions on the activities of peasants
C. allowed some capitalist enterprise
D. was continued by Stalin

Ans: C
Diff: M
Page: 675

42. Stalin's agricultural policy consisted of all of the following, except:
A. importing grain from Western Europe
B. suppressing the kulaks
C. collectivizing agriculture
D. mechanizing agriculture

Ans: A
Diff: E
Page: 676

43. Women in the Soviet Union:
A. received equal pay for equal work
B. were granted maternity leave with full pay
C. were generally shut out of the professions
D. had a worse legal position than the women of most Western European countries

Ans: B
Diff: M
Page: 677

44. T F Lenin felt that the common working people should lead the communist revolution.

Ans: F
Diff: M
Page: 674

45. T F The Czar's establishment of a *duma* hastened the coming Bolshevik Revolution.

Ans: F
Diff: H
Page: 674

46. T F Although it was not enforced, the Soviet government did mandate equal pay for equal work.

Ans: T
Diff: E
Page: 677

47. Describe the major events of 1917 and 1918 in Russia, including those that led to the Bolshevik seizure of power and also the major policies of the revolutionaries immediately after seizing power.

Diff: M
Pages: 674-675

48. First describe the nature of Russian agriculture and industry prior to the Bolshevik Revolution; then describe and analyze the agricultural and industrial policies of Lenin and Stalin.

Diff: H
Pages: 673-677

49. A constitutional amendment granted American women the right to vote in:
A. 1930
B. 1920
C. 1929
D. 1915

Ans: B
Diff: E
Page: 679

50. Which of the following groups was NOT a target of the Ku Klux Klan in the 1920s?
A. Jews
B. African Americans
C. Protestants
D. Catholics

Ans: C
Diff: M
Page: 680

51. The Great Depression:
A. led the United States to forgive loans owed it by European countries
B. led many countries to impose import restrictions
C. was caused by government over-regulation of the economy
D. resulted in a huge increase in food prices

Ans: B
Diff: M
Page: 680

52. Of the following countries, this one was affected least by the Great Depression:
A. United States
B. Argentina
C. Italy
D. Soviet Union

Ans: D
Diff: M
Page: 680

53. During the 1920s and early 1930s, Germany:
A. suffered a major deflation of its currency
B. had reverted back to an authoritarian form of government
C. had suffered severe economic hardship from the payment of war reparations
D. rearmed itself and seized the Rhineland

Ans: C
Diff: M
Page: 682

54. T F The United States refused to join the League of Nations.

Ans: T
Diff: E
Page: 679

55. T F The Eighteenth Amendment to the U.S. Constitution granted women the right to vote.

Ans: F
Diff: M
Page: 679

56. T F The Civilian Conservation Corps provided jobs to about 3 million young men.

Ans: T
Diff: E
Page: 681

57. T F The American Social Security Act of 1935 offered unemployment, old age, and disability insurance long before it was available in Western Europe.

Ans: F
Diff: M
Page: 681

58. What were the economic and political results of the Great Depression?

Diff: M
Pages: 680-681

59. How did President Franklin D. Roosevelt respond to the Great Depression? In what areas of social welfare did he seek to use the government, and in what specific ways?

Diff: M
Page: 681

60. Describe the vision of the twentieth century presented by Polish poet Wislawa Szymborska. How does she suggest the world respond?

Diff: M
Page: 681

1. Fascism does NOT stand for:
A. individual rights
B. the supremacy of the national leader
C. the importance of nationalism
D. a willingness to use violence and intimidation

Ans: A
Diff: E
Page: 686

2. Which of the following was NOT a tactic utilized by Mussolini in his efforts to claim power in Italy?
A. violence
B. fraud
C. rational debate
D. intimidation

Ans: C
Diff: M
Page: 686

3. The League of Nations responded to Mussolini's invasion of Ethiopia by:
A. doing almost nothing
B. sending troops in League forces to drive the Italians out of Ethiopia
C. imposing sanctions on Italy
D. trying Mussolini for war crimes

Ans: A
Diff: M
Page: 687

4. Adolf Hitler:
A. opposed German nationalism
B. learned about fascism from Benito Mussolini
C. laid out his political program in *Mein Kampf*
D. came to power in a military coup

Ans: C
Diff: M
Page: 688

5. Which of the following is NOT a reason why the German people tolerated Hitler's leadership during the mid-1930s?
A. Hitler's use of the SS made opposition to his policies a risky stance to take
B. His policies brought some measure of economic stability to the impoverished country
C. His military policies offered a sense of security
D. His persecution of the Jews purged Germany of a legitimate threat to national security

Ans: D
Diff: M
Pages: 689-690

6. In Japan in the 1920s:
A. urbanization decreased
B. labor organization was ruthlessly suppressed
C. economic growth rates slowed to less than 2 percent per year
D. the populace became politicized

Ans: D
Diff: M
Page: 691

7. In the 1930s, the Japanese military:
A. was required by the Constitution to have at least two of its members in the government's cabinet
B. had a decreasing role in the politics of Japan
C. refrained from any provocative actions abroad
D. declined in prestige in Japan

Ans: A
Diff: M
Page: 692

8. T F Hitler's rise to become chancellor was entirely legal.

Ans: T
Diff: M
Page: 688

9. T F The *Gestapo* was established in 1936 to eliminate (through murder or internment) opposition leaders who advocated anti-Hitler ideologies.

Ans: T
Diff: E
Page: 689

10. T F Japan had a high rate of economic growth during the two decades preceding World War II.

Ans: T
Diff: E
Page: 691

11. T F The *zaibatsu* was an ancient craft guild that had renewed popularity in Japan during the 1920s.

Ans: F
Diff: M
Page: 691

12. Define fascism and contrast the fascist government of Mussolini with that of Hitler. Explain why you think so many people supported their policies.

Diff: M
Pages: 686-689

13. Describe the economic and political conditions that led Germany to select Adolf Hitler as its leader. Include in your essay a discussion of Hitler's principle beliefs.

Diff: M
Pages: 687-89

14. The League of Nations:
A. had several early successes
B. was essentially a tool of the United States, since it was the most powerful member
C. was a forum for resolving international conflicts through negotiations
D. forced Italy to withdraw its military from Ethiopia

Ans: C
Diff: M
Page: 692

15. Which of the following did NOT support General Francisco Franco during the Spanish Civil War?
A. Germany
B. Italy
C. Soviet Union
D. the Spanish clergy

Ans: C
Diff: M
Page: 694

16. Which of the following territories was annexed by Germany when Hitler declared an Anschluss of the two countries.
A. Poland
B. Czechoslovakia
C. Italy
D. Austria

Ans: D
Diff: E
Page: 695

17. Hitler invaded which of the following on 1 September 1939, sparking World War II?
A. Austria
B. Czechoslovakia
C. Poland
D. France

Ans: C
Diff: E
Page: 696

18. Which country experienced the most dramatic increase in their defense expenditures from 1930 to 1938?
A. Germany
B. Japan
C. USA
D. Britain

Ans: A
Diff: M
Page: 696

19. In 1925, France pledged to protect both Poland and Czechoslovakia in case of any future attack.

Ans: T
Diff: E
Page: 693

20. T F Nazi Germany supported the Republicans in the Spanish Civil War.

Ans: F
Diff: M
Page: 694

21. T F World War II started when Germany invaded Czechoslovakia.

Ans: F
Diff: E
Page: 695

22. T F World War II ended in Europe before it was over in the Pacific.

Ans: T
Diff: E
Page: 695

23. T F The democratic countries of Europe did little to stop Hitler prior to the outbreak of World War II.

Ans: T
Diff: M
Page: 695

24. Explain why Germany was able to gain control over the Rhineland, the Sudetenland, and Austria without firing a shot.

Diff: M
Page: 695

25. After signing the Nazi-Soviet pact, the Soviet Union engaged in its own aggressive expansion. Describe those actions and evaluate the threat they posed to world peace.

Diff: M
Page: 696

26. Which of the following aggressive actions occurred before World War II had officially begun?
A. Japan conquered Burma
B. German forces invaded the Soviet Union
C. Japan bombed Pearl Harbor
D. Japan invaded China

Ans: D
Diff: M
Page: 695

27. Which of the following was NOT a part of the famed "Maginot Line"?
A. defended trenches
B. elevated gun turrets
C. underground bunkers
D. minefields

Ans: B
Diff: M
Page: 697

28. Which of the following was NOT a part of Japan's "Greater East Asia Co-Prosperity Sphere"?
A. open trade with the West
B. sources of raw materials for Japanese industries
C. markets for Japanese products
D. exportation of Japanese culture

Ans: A
Diff: M
Page: 700

29. In 1941, 2 million Serbs and other "undesirables" were murdered by:
A. the Nazis
B. the Japanese
C. the Ustasa
D. the Soviets

Ans: C
Diff: M
Page: 701

30. The turning point in the Eastern front came at the battle of:
A. Leningrad
B. Stalingrad
C. Moscow
D. Kursk

Ans: B
Diff: E
Page: 701

31. The first atomic bomb was dropped on:
A. Hiroshima
B. Nagasaki
C. Marshall Islands
D. Tokyo

Ans: A
Diff: E
Page: 703

32. This event was most responsible for the Japanese decision to surrender in World War II:
A. the firebombing of Tokyo and other large cities
B. the dropping of atomic bombs on Hiroshima and Nagasaki
C. the defeat of Germany
D. the depletion of its oil supplies

Ans: B
Diff: E
Page: 708

33. T F In the "Rape of Nanjing," Japanses soldiers utilized brutal tactics and committed atrocities against Chinese civilians.

Ans: T
Diff: E
Page: 699

34. The Soviet Union suffered the highest casualty rate in World War II: about 20 million.

Ans: T
Diff: E
Page: 705

35. T F Women did much of the factory work in America during World War II.

Ans: T
Diff: E
Page: 706

36. T F Hitler believed in a racial hierarchy and placed blacks at the bottom.

Ans: F
Diff: M
Page: 707

37. What were the important events in Japanese foreign and military policy between 1930 and 1945? What were the major reasons for Japan's defeat in World War II?

Diff: M
Pages: 699-705

38. What were the four main goals of the American occupation force in Japan? What specific steps were taken to achieve them?

Diff: M
Pages: 703-705

39. In 1942 Axis power extended as far east as:
A. the Volga
B. the Danube
C. Pyrenees
D. Finland

Ans: A
Diff: M
Page: 697

40. Which of the following was NOT included in the "Greater East Asia Co-Prosperity Sphere" by 1942?
A. Guam
B. Palau
C. Fiji
D. Iwo Jima

Ans: C
Diff: M
Page: 704

41. Which of the following achieved the highest level of aircraft production by 1944?
A. USA
B. USSR
C. Germany
D. Japan

Ans: A
Diff: E
Page: 705

42. Kim Young-shil testified about her experiences as one of Japan's "comfort women" during World War II. Describe the impact this had on the women, and explain the manner in which they have subsequently been treated by Japanese authorities.

Diff: M
Page: 707

43. Psychologist Stanley Milgram attempted to explain why German soldiers followed orders to commit genocide. Outline Milgram's experience and evaluate the validity of his findings. Do you think this was an ethical experiment?

Diff: M
Page: 709

44. Mohandas Gandhi argued that
A. the pursuit of material comfort was the path to enlightenment
B. the civilization was on the path to self-destruction
C. technology offered salvation to enslaved laborers throughout the world
D. European political systems were superior

Ans: B
Diff: M
Page: 710

45. The United Nations:
A. was founded in 1919
B. had over 120 members by 1947
C. was envisioned primarily as a vehicle to promote peace
D. admitted the People's Republic of China shortly after the completion of the Chinese communist revolution

Ans: C
Diff: E
Page: 715

46. This is NOT a United Nations agency:
A. International Monetary Fund
B. World Health Organization
C. Food and Agriculture Organization
D. International Labor Organization

Ans: A
Diff: M
Page: 715

47. All of the following were consequences of the American occupation of Japan, except:
A. freedom of speech
B. universal adult suffrage
C. demobilization of the military
D. the keeping of the emperor as the spiritual head of the country

Ans: D
Diff: M
Page: 717

48. The Marshall Plan accomplished all the following in Western Europe, except:
A. expedite Europe's economic recovery
B. lead to détente with the Soviet Union
C. create new markets for American goods
D. reduce the threat of communist takeover

Ans: B
Diff: M
Page: 719

49. T F Elie Wiesel was awarded the Nobel Peace Prize for his efforts to inform the world about the potential destructiveness of humans.

Ans: T
Diff: M
Page: 713

50. T F By 1950, Japan had become an American ally in the Cold War.

Ans: T
Diff: E
Page: 717

51. T F The Truman Doctrine offered to extend assistance to help any free people resist capitalist imperialism.

Ans: F
Diff: M
Page: 719

52. T F The Warsaw Pact was established in response to the creation of NATO.

Ans: T
Diff: E
Page: 720

53. Describe the reaction of writers and artists to World War II; particularly to the holocaust. What conclusions did they draw about the fate of civilization?

Diff: M
Pages: 710-714

54. Explain why the Soviets blockaded Berlin. How did the Americans respond, and what did this portend about the future relationship between the Soviets and the United States?

Diff: M
Page: 719

55. What were the causes of the Cold War? Was there any way in which the conflict could have been avoided?

Diff: M
Pages: 719-720

56. Present and analyze the arguments for and against the use of atomic weapons on Japan.

Diff: M
Page: 712

57. Which of the following was NOT a member of NATO?
A. France
B. West Germany
C. Turkey
D. Austria

Ans: D
Diff: E
Page: 714

58. Which of the following was NOT a member of the Warsaw Pact?
A. Bulgaria
B. Albania
C. Switzerland
D. Romania

Ans: C
Diff: E
Page: 714

59. Which of the following was NOT one of the aims of the United Nations according to the preamble of their charter?
A. promote the economic and social advancement of all people
B. maintain international peace and security
C. promote social progress
D. establish democratic governments throughout the world

Ans: D
Diff: M
Page: 715

60. T F According to the preamble to the charter of the United Nations, the world is encouraged to practice tolerance.

Ans: T
Diff: E
Page: 715

1. Between 1945 and 1948, the Soviet Union imposed communist governments on all but which one of the following?
A. Romania
B. Bulgaria
C. Poland
D. West Germany

Ans: D
Diff: E
Page: 726

2. The Korean War drove a wedge between the United States and many of its European allies because:
A. the American drive into North Korea was costly, belligerent, and provoked the Chinese
B. the Americans refused to accept assistance from the allies
C. the Americans wanted to push into China to route communism
D. the war took American attention and resources away from the situation in Europe

Ans: A
Diff: E
Page: 729

3. Nikita Khruschev:
A. was a zombie-like person who showed no emotion
B. put more people in prison than Stalin did
C. publicly denounced Stalin
D. won a stand-off with the United States during the 1962 Cuban Missile Crisis

Ans: C
Diff: E
Page: 729

4. In Central America, the US and the USSR supported opposing parties in guerrilla wars in all of the following countries, except:
A. Colombia
B. Guatemala
C. Nicaragua
D. El Salvador

Ans: A
Diff: M
Page: 732

5. Which of the following actions was NOT taken by Fidel Castro after he took power?
A. the expropriation of foreign assets
B. the collectivization of farms
C. the allocation of funds and energies to health, education, and cultural activities
D. redistributed land to individual peasant families

Ans: D
Diff: M
Page: 733

6. This event brought the USSR and the United States the closest to nuclear war:

A. North Korea's invasion of South Korea
B. American involvement in the Vietnam War
C. the American invasion of Cambodia
D. the placement of Soviet nuclear missiles in Cuba

Ans: D
Diff: M
Page: 733

7. T F The Korean War provided a significant economic boost for Japan.

Ans: T
Diff: E
Page: 728

8. T F Dwight Eisenhower felt that the military-industrial complex was America's best guarantee of freedom.

Ans: F
Diff: M
Page: 731

9. T F Che Guevara was exiled from Cuba by Fidel Castro after a power struggle.

Ans: F
Diff: M
Page: 733

10. Define "proxy war" and explain how the Cold War erupted into heated conflicts in the client states. What impact did these wars have on the relationship between the US and the USSR?

Diff: M
Page: 732

11. What were the social accomplishments of the Cuban Revolution? What classes benefited the most from Castro's rule?

Diff: M
Page: 733

12. Which nation had the largest defense expenditure in 1987?
A. USA
B. USSR
C. China
D. Germany

Ans: A
Diff: E
Page: 732

13. Which country witnessed the greatest decrease in their expenditures from 1987 to 1997?
A. USA
B. USSR
C. China
D. Germany

Ans: B
Diff: E
Page: 732

14. T F Che Guevara's speeches and writings against imperialism inspired guerrilla movements throughout the world.

Ans: T
Diff: E
Page: 734

15. The United States threatened to cut off Marshall Plan aid to which of the following to force them to withdraw from Indonesia?
A. the French
B. the Dutch
C. the English
D. the Japanese

Ans: B
Diff: E
Page: 736

16. Initially, the United States got involved in Vietnam to support:
A. the South Vietnamese
B. the Vietminh
C. the Vietcong
D. the French

Ans: A
Diff: M
Page: 736

17. Gamal Abdel Nasser:
A. was strongly in the Western camp during the Cold War
B. nationalized the Suez Canal
C. opposed the formation of non-aligned nations organizations
D. was unpopular both in Egypt and in the Arab world

Ans: B
Diff: E
Page: 737

18. The Algerian Revolution:
A. nearly caused a civil war in France
B. was led by a large class of university-educated Arab elites
C. was followed by similar uprisings in Morocco and Tunisia
D. cost very few lives

Ans: A
Diff: M
Page: 740

19. Portugal's colonies were given their independence in 1975 primarily because:
A. Portugal could no longer afford to fight the war
B. the Portuguese dictator had been overthrown by democratic forces
C. the United Nations had imposed sanctions on Portugal
D. the Soviet Union threatened to attack Portugal if it did not grant independence

Ans: B
Diff: H
Page: 742

20. T F Decolonization was in part a consequence of the world wars and the global depression.

Ans: T
Diff: E
Page: 734

21. T F When the United States left Vietnam, the communists were defeated.

Ans: F
Diff: M
Page: 737

22. T F Upon gaining independence, Congo/Zaire had a large and well-educated elite ready to guide the new nation.

Ans: F
Diff: H
Page: 740

23. Describe the domestic and international policies of Gamal Abdel Nasser. What tarnished his reputation near the end of his rule?

Diff: M
Page: 738

24. Both Vietnam and Algeria were colonies of France. Compare and contrast the decolonization process in Vietnam with that in Algeria.

Diff: M
Pages: 738-741

25. Contrast the various interpretations of the impact of colonial rule on developing nations. Describe the benefits and the drawbacks of colonization. Overall, would you say the impact was more positive or more negative? Explain.

Diff: M
Page: 739

26. Which of the following African countries had the greatest gross national product in 1994:
A. South Africa
B. Zimbabwe
C. Congo
D. Algeria

Ans: A
Diff: E
Page: 742

27. Of the following, which was NOT one of the third world leaders to organize the Bandung Conference?
A. Jawaharlal Nehru
B. Gamal Abdel Nasser
C. Zhou Enlai
D. Marshal Tito

Ans: C
Diff: E
Page: 745

28. Colonel Jacobo Arbenz of Guatemala:
A. turned to the Soviet Union for arms and aid almost immediately after coming to power
B. wanted to force United Fruit Company to sell land to the government for the declared value on tax statements
C. wanted to make his country more dependent on United States businesses
D. lost power in a free and democratic election

Ans: B
Diff: M
Page: 748

29. Rigoberta Menchu:
A. took up arms against the Guatemalan government
B. wrote an international bestseller when she was in her 60s
C. moved to Spain in the mid-1980s
D. won the Nobel Peace Prize

Ans: D
Diff: E
Page: 748

30. Chile's Salvador Allende:
A. was a Christian Democrat
B. came to power by extra-constitutional means
C. was overthrown with the help of the United States Central Intelligence Agency
D. went into exile in Spain after losing power

Ans: C
Diff: M
Page: 749

31. Of the following sectors of Iranian society, which was least opposed to the Shah?
A. intellectuals
B. students
C. the *ulama*
D. business elites

Ans: D
Diff: M
Page: 750

32. The Ayatollah Khomeini:
A. opposed rule by Islamic law
B. opposed the seizure of the American embassy in Tehran
C. spent many years in exile
D. sought to form an alliance with the government of Saudi Arabia

Ans: C
Diff: M
Page: 750

33. T F The term "Third World" has many negative connotations and thus is resented by those whom it is used to describe.

Ans: T
Diff: E
Page: 743

34. T F Despite what the US believed, not every communist country was aligned with the Soviet Union.

Ans: T
Diff: M
Page: 746

35. T F Most borders in Africa reflect the boundaries between ethnic groups and tribes.

Ans: F
Diff: M
Page: 743

36. T F The Sandinistas' revolt helped bring the Samoza government to power in Nicaragua.

Ans: F
Diff: M
Page: 747

37. Describe the rise and fall of Salvador Allende in Chile. Who supported him? Who opposed him? What were the economic and political results of his overthrow?

Diff: M
Page: 749

38. First describe and analyze the policies of Shah Muhammad Reza Pavlavi in Iran. Then discuss who those policies alienated and how this laid the groundwork for the 1979 revolution. Follow this with an elucidation of the policies of Ayatollah Khomeini.

Diff: H
Pages: 749-750

39. Of the following countries, which won independence first?
A. Togo
B. Malawi
C. Mozambique
D. Namibia

Ans: A
Diff: M
Page: 744

40. Of the following, which was NOT one of the three major stages of development for the United Nations?
A. dominance of the agenda by former colonies
B. forum for international action in regional conflicts
C. mediation of the Cold War
D. initiator of programs to bring about global economic equality

Ans: D
Diff: M
Page: 752

41. To the best of medical experts' knowledge, this disease has been totally eradicated:
A. smallpox
B. malaria
C. yellow fever
D. mad cow disease

Ans: A
Diff: E
Page: 753

42. Human population:
A. grew at a faster rate in the 1990s than in the 1960s
B. just recently reached the level it was at in 1914
C. is currently over 6 billion
D. has reached a steady state in which it is neither increasing or decreasing

Ans: C
Diff: E
Page: 754

43. The oil shock of 1973:
A. had little effect on Japan, since it imported little oil from the Middle East
B. caused Japan to focus its attention on increasing energy-intensive industries
C. encouraged Japan to be more energy efficient
D. resulted in a sharp increase of economic growth for Japan

Ans: C
Diff: M
Page: 758

44. Between 1952 and 1973, the Japanese government did NOT:
A. regulate national tax policies
B. regulate national investment policies
C. encourage capitalist free-market competition
D. provide funds for investment in industry

Ans: C
Diff: M
Page: 759

45. Which of the following was NOT a result of the 1973 OPEC oil embargo?
A. prices quadrupled
B. the lack of energy caused many industries to lay off workers
C. energy-efficient machinery was developed
D. Western nations imposed economic sanctions on OPEC members

Ans: D
Diff: M
Page: 761

46. Which of following was part of the original purview of the United Nations?
A. conflict resolution
B. human rights
C. peace keeping
D. international law

Ans: B
Diff: M
Page: 763

47. T F The "population bomb" was balanced by an overall decline in birth rates at the end of the twentieth century.

Ans: T
Diff: M
Page: 755

48. T F The Asian tigers were successful primarily because they did NOT follow Japan's pattern of development.

Ans: F
Diff: M
Page: 759

49. T F The primary goal of the World Bank was to provide the funds for reconstruction in war torn nations.

Ans: T
Diff: E
Page: 761

50. T F Transnational corporations operate in many countries with no clear headquarters.

Ans: T
Diff: E
Page: 761

51. T F the 1973 "oil shock" was OPEC's reaction to the American support of Israel in the Yom Kippur War.

Ans: T
Diff: E
Page: 761

52. Why have the Asian tigers had such phenomenal rates of economic growth? Why did they experience economic downturn in the late 1990s?

Diff: M
Page: 759

53. Describe the program developed at Bretton Woods in 1944. What new institutions did it create? Evaluate their success.

Diff: M
Pages: 759-761

54. Describe how OPEC's manipulations of oil prices have adversely affected most third world's nations.

Diff: M
Page: 761

55. Which of the following United Nations agencies oversees international trade?
A. UNESCO
B. WHO
C. WTO
D. ILO

Ans: C
Diff: E
Page: 752

56. DDT:
A. was useless in slowing the spread of malaria
B. is still widely in use in Western countries
C. was toxic to animals
D. was not toxic to humans

Ans: C
Diff: M
Page: 753

57. Explain Rachel Carson's position on the health of the environment. What did she see as the greatest problem and in what ways did people respond to her concerns?

Diff: M
Page: 753

58. T F The nuclear reactor at Three Mile Island, Pennsylvania experienced a partial melt-down in 1979.

Ans: F
Diff: M
Page: 755

59. T F the nuclear power plant at Chernobyl experienced a partial melt-down in 1986.

Ans: T
Diff: E
Page: 758

60. Explain the relationship between technology and ethics as described by E.F. Schumacher. Do you agree with his perspective? Explain.

Diff: M
Page: 760

1. Population density is highest in:
A. Europe
B. China
C. North America
D. South America

Ans: B
Diff: E
Page: 767

2. China:
A. had no powerful central government for most of the first half of the twentieth century
B. is culturally very diverse
C. was a country at peace until the invasion of Japan
D. became a communist state in the late 1950s

Ans: A
Diff: E
Page: 767

3. India:
A. had no real sense of unity during the first half of the twentieth century
B. chose democracy after it became independent
C. has pursued free-market economics
D. has an ethnically homogeneous population

Ans: B
Diff: E
Page: 767

4. Chiang Kai-shek:
A. was too young to fight in the 1911 revolution
B. was a strong supporter of industrial workers
C. assumed the leadership of the Guomindang (GMD)
D. fought ceaselessly against Mao's forces

Ans: C
Diff: M
Page: 769

5. Chiang maintained close ties with all of the following, except:
A. mobsters
B. western businessmen
C. Comintern agents
D. leaders of western European nations

Ans: D
Diff: H
Page: 769

6. Mao:
A. was too young to participate in the 1911 revolution
B. traveled widely in Europe and the United States
C. grew up in an upper-middle class household in Shanghai
D. became interested in communism while a college student

Ans: D
Diff: M
Page: 771

7. Mao felt that this class was the most important for the communist revolution in China:
A. workers
B. warlords
C. businessmen
D. peasants

Ans: D
Diff: E
Page: 772

8. During his first years in the communist party, Mao:
A. had doubts about the necessity of a violent revolution
B. flirted with the idea of joining Guomindang
C. worked with peasants in Hunan
D. traveled to Moscow for Comintern meetings

Ans: C
Diff: M
Page: 772

9. Mao's guerrilla fighting tactics did NOT include this:
A. "the enemy advances, we retreat"
B. "the enemy camps, we rest"
C. the enemy tires, we attack"
D. the enemy retreats, we pursue"

Ans: B
Diff: M
Page: 773

10. Mao's views on women included the idea that women should:
A. stay at home and raise large families
B. have a lot more authority within the family
C. gain husbands through arranged marriages
D. not work in factories

Ans: B
Diff: M
Page: 773

11. During the revolution, the Chinese communist program included all of the following, except:
A. an industrially-based economy
B. a benevolent communist leadership
C. increased literacy
D. paramedics for health care

Ans: A
Diff: M
Page: 774

12. In China after 1945:
A. the Chinese communists retreated to near the northern border of China
B. Chiang's forces fought professionally and made many gains
C. the United States provided military aid and logistical support to Chiang's troops
D. Hong Kong declared its independence from China

Ans: C
Diff: M
Page: 775

13. Early policies of the Chinese communists after gaining power in 1949 did NOT include:
A. large-scale industrial activities
B. redistribution of land
C. women's rights to hold land
D. universal literacy

Ans: A
Diff: M
Page: 776

14. In the area of foreign relations, China has:
A. typically had good relations with the USSR
B. refused to get involved in leftist insurgencies in other countries
C. refused to join the UN
D. asserted its right to have nuclear weapons

Ans: D
Diff: E
Page: 777

15. The Great Leap Forward:
A. sent millions of peasants to the cities
B. ended with Mao calling for the blooming of a hundred flowers
C. led to death by starvation for millions
D. was opposed by Mao

Ans: C
Diff: M
Page: 778

16. The Cultural Revolution:
A. began in 1957
B. was carried out primarily by the Red Guard
C. was focused primarily on the peasants
D. led to the further entrenchment of party bureaucrats

Ans: B
Diff: M
Page: 779

17. T F Both China and India are heavily urbanized countries.

Ans: F
Diff: E
Page: 767

18. T F Mao felt that violence was usually necessary to seize political power.

Ans: T
Diff: E
Page: 772

19. T F By the fall of 1949, the Guomindang had been driven out of mainland China to the island of Taiwan.

Ans: T
Diff: E
Page: 776

20. T F China liberated Tibet in 1950, allowing Tibetan Buddhism to flourish.

Ans: F
Diff: M
Page: 781

21. T F China supported the government of Khmer Rouge in Cambodia.

Ans: T
Diff: E
Page: 781

22. Describe and analyze Mao's philosophy of revolution. Was it applicable to China? Would it have been applicable to Britain or the United States?

Diff: M
Pages: 771-772

23. What were the policies of the Soviets set up by Mao and his supporters during the revolution?

Diff: M
Pages: 776-777

24. Compare, contrast, and analyze the three main phases of China's post-revolution economy: 1949-1957, the Great Leap Forward, major reform after 1970.

Diff: H
Pages: 776-779

25. Describe the reasons for the Cultural Revolution, who carried it out, and who its targets were.

Diff: E
Pages: 778-779

26. Describe the major aspects of Chinese foreign policy since 1949, including relations with the United States, the USSR, and India.

Diff: M
Pages: 779-781

27. Which of the following has the least dense concentration of population?
A. China
B. India
C. South America
D. Australia

Ans: D
Diff: E
Page: 768

28. Which of the following programs occurred first?
A. "100 Flowers Campaign"
B. "Great Leap Forward"
C. "Quit India"
D. Chinese expulsion of foreigners

Ans: C
Diff. M
Page: 770

29. Which region of China was occupied by Japan by 1933?
A. Manchuria
B. Shanxi
C. Shandong
D. Taiwan

Ans: A
Diff: M
Page: 775

30. How did journalist Liu Binyan view Mao's "Hundred Flowers" Campaign?   Why did his views change over time and in what ways?

Diff: M
Page: 778

31. Late nineteenth and early twentieth century British rule in India included this policy:
A. creation of the Indian National Congress
B. suppression of all expressions of Indian nationalism
C. complete independence for India by 1940
D. preventing the creation of a British-educated Indian elite

Ans: A
Diff: M
Page: 782

32. The Government of India Act of 1919 called for:
A. the abolition of provincial legislatures
B. a massive literacy campaign for the lower classes
C. creation of a dual government
D. consolidation of political power entirely within the British colonial administration system

Ans: C
Diff: M
Page: 783

33. Gandhi:
A. was born into the untouchables caste
B. lived in South Africa for about 20 years
C. never went to college
D. was more famous for his legal skills than his political skills

Ans: B
Diff: E
Page: 783

34. Gandhi's desires for India included all of the following, except:
A. pride in Indian civilization
B. the use of indigenous products
C. large-scale industrialization
D. independence from Britain

Ans: C
Diff: M
Page: 785

35. Gandhi was most successful in converting these people to his political program:
A. rural Hindus
B. the residents of Bengal
C. left-wing socialists
D. the followers of Mohammed Ali Jinnah

Ans: A
Diff: M
Page: 786

36. India's pre-independence Muslims:
A. favored political association with the Hindu majority
B. wanted a secular state
C. were concentrated in the southern tip of the subcontinent
D. were concerned about protecting their rights

Ans: D
Diff: M
Page: 786

37. Of the following, which was NOT one of the five principal domestic programs Gandhi saw as central to India's development?
A. Hindu-Muslim unity
B. prohibition of alcohol
C. maintenance of traditional caste distinctions and rules
D. small-scale, labor-intensive technologies

Ans: C
Diff: E
Page: 786

38. The official language(s) of India is/are:
A. English
B. Hindi
C. Vernacular languages
D. English and Hindi

39. Which of the following was NOT boycotted by the non-cooperation campaign of 1920-22?
A. British colonial schools
B. British manufactures
C. indigenous products
D. British law courts

40. To force Britain to grant independence, the "Quit India" campaign involved:
A. withdrawing Indian political support of Britain in World War II
B. boycotting all British imports
C. widespread civil disobedience
D. armed insurrection against the British colonial government

41. In the immediate aftermath of Indian independence, all of the following happened, except:
A. the loss of territory on the north to China
B. the creation of Pakistan
C. the assumption of power by the Congress party
D. the relinquishing of local power by Indian princes

42. Women in India:
A. cannot marry until they are eighteen
B. are prohibited from serving in legislatures
C. cannot divorce their husbands if they are Hindus
D. number substantially fewer than men

43. The Green Revolution included ample production of all of the following except:
A. wheat & grains
B. rice & grains
C. corn & beans
D. wheat & rice

44. Which of the following problems was NOT associated with the agricultural revolutions?
A. fears that the new levels of production would lead to another population explosion
B. increase in the gap between the rich and the poor
C. fears that the newly developed seeds were not genetically diverse enough
D. fears that the massive amounts of chemical fertilizers would ruin the ecology

Ans: A
Diff: M
Page: 795

45. This country used forced sterilization as a form of family planning:
A. China
B. India
C. Iran
D. Soviet Union

Ans: B
Diff: E
Page: 796

46. Which of the following was NOT part of Nehru's industrial policy?
A. central planning
B. regulation of the large-scale capitalist sector
C. handicraft production
D. industrialization

Ans: C
Diff: E
Page: 796

47. A generation after ending colonialism, which of the following accomplishments is NOT shared by China and India?
A. cumulative and growing economic expansion
B. political cohesion
C. social transformation
D. concentration on urban areas

Ans: D
Diff: M
Page: 798

48. T F Gandhi's teachings promoted passive resistance.

Ans: T
Diff: M
Page: 784

49. T F Gandhi's activities in South Africa earned him the esteem of his countrymen in South Africa and in India.

Ans: T
Diff: H
Page: 785

50. T F Gandhi struggled to end discrimination against the untouchables class.

Ans: T
Diff: E
Page: 786

51. T F Pakistan consisted of territorial "wings" on the west and east sides of India.

Ans: T
Diff: E
Page: 790

52. T F Domination of Indian politics by the Congress party ended with the assassination of Rajiv Gandhi.

Ans: T
Diff: M
Page: 793

53. T F India is still not capable of supplying all its own food.

Ans: F
Diff: M
Page: 795

54. Describe Gandhi's philosophy of the uses of non-violence.

Diff: E
Pages: 783-785

55. Compare the views of Gandhi and Nehru on the use of technology and large-scale economic production in India.

Diff: E
Pages: 788, 796

56. What type of government does India have, and what are its key characteristics in terms of institutions, civil liberties, and economic policies?

Diff: M
Pages: 792-793

57 Describe the major aspects of India's foreign policy since gaining independence.

Diff: M
Page: 797

58. This important figure in the struggle for Indian independence was also a poet and a musician:
A. Jawaharlal Nehru
B. Muhammad Ali Jinnah
C. Subhas Chandra Bose
D. Rabindranath Tagore

Ans: D
Diff: M
Page: 782

59. Jawaharlal Nehru:
A. was assassinated by a Hindu extremist
B. was right-wing in his economic thinking
C. served as prime minister of India for over a decade
D. had a lot of personal animosity toward Gandhi

Ans: C
Diff: E
Page: 782

60. How does Gandhi portray his experience with racism in South Africa? What was his response to the situation he describes?

Diff: E
Page: 784

61. What changes does Gandhi propose for industrial laborers? How does this position conflict with his attitude toward technology?

Diff: M
Page: 788

62. T F Bangladesh was part of Pakistan after 1947 until gaining its independence in 1971.

Ans: T
Diff: E
Page: 790

63. T F Pakistan was separated from India in 1947 because the majority of the population was Muslim rather than Hindu.

Ans: T
Diff: E
Page: 790

64. T F Union Carbide corporation willingly compensated the victims of the 1984 explosion at their insecticide plant in Bhopal.

Ans: F
Diff: E
Page: 797

Part 8: Evolving Identities (1979 – Present)

1. Which of the following is NOT a true statement about the United States?
A. it is a constitutional democracy
B. it protects the public welfare
C. it has always provided democracy and freedom for all
D. it protects private property

Ans: C
Diff: M
Page: 804

2. New challenges facing the post-Cold War world include all of the following except:
A. AIDS
B. trafficking of women and children
C. trafficking of human organs
D. the imperialism of the Soviet Union

Ans: D
Diff: E
Page: 805

3 T F Although the United States claims to protect private property, it has enacted important laws restricting that protection if it is necessary for the public good.

Ans: T
Diff: E
Page: 504

4. T F The illegal trafficking of drugs is no longer a significant global problem.

Ans: F
Diff: M
Page: 805

5. Explain how evolving identities present new challenges for nations today.

Diff: M
Pages: 804-805

Political Identities

1. Mikhail Gorbachev:
A. refused to reduce his country's nuclear arsenal
B. was removed from power by a military coup
C. was more successful at *glasnost* then at *perestroika*
D. kept tight control over Eastern Europe

Ans: C
Diff: H
Page: 808

2. Which of the following was encompassed in Gorbachev's policy of *glasnost*?
A. the revelation of Stalin's atrocities
B. reducing the size of the bureaucracy
C. competitive economic planning
D. reforming centralized planning of the economy

Ans: A
Diff: M
Page: 808

3. Boris Yeltsin:
A. reversed much of the economic privatization of the Gorbachev era
B. lost a presidential election in 1996
C. managed to keep Ukraine, Belarus, and the Baltic states under the political control of Russia
D. created the Commonwealth of Independent States

Ans: D
Diff: M
Page: 811

4. During the 1990s, the gross domestic product of Russia
A. maintained an even position
B. dropped by 50 percent
C. grew by 50 percent
D. dropped by one third

Ans: B
Diff: E
Page: 811

5. During the early 1990s, the American economy entered a new phase of growth led by
A. innovations in biotechnology
B. innovations in heavy manufacturing
C. innovations in communications and technology
D. dramatic increase in demand for service sector workers

Ans: C
Diff: E
Page: 813

6. Which of the following did NOT join NATO during the 1990s?
A. Czech Republic
B. Hungary
C. Poland
D. Saudi Arabia

Ans: D
Diff: M
Page: 813

7. Timothy McVeigh perpetrated this incident of domestic terrorism in 1995
A. first World Trade Center bombing
B. the attack on the USS Cole
C. the bombing of the federal building in Oklahoma City
D. the bombing of the US embassy in Beirut

Ans: C
Diff: E
Page: 814

8. T F The economic restructuring of the Soviet Union was called *perestroika*.

Ans: T
Diff: E
Page: 808

9. T F The return of capitalism to Russia coincided with a significant increase in crime.

Ans: T
Diff: M
Page: 811

10. T F Russia willingly granted independence to Chechnya in 1994.

Ans: F
Diff: M
Page: 811

11. T F The East-West division of Europe began to erode as many former Soviet satellite countries joined the European Union.

Ans: T
Diff: E
Page: 812

12. Describe and analyze the situation Mikhail Gorbachev faced as leader of the Soviet Union, both domestically and internationally. What were his main economic, political, and foreign policies, and how well did they work? Did Boris Yeltsin continue with these policies?

Diff: H
Pages: 808-809

13. Describe and analyze the changes in that occurred in the United States after the fall of the Soviet Union. How did this affect the international position of the United States?

Diff: H
Page: 813

14. Which of the following newly independent nations shares a border with Afghanistan?
A. Kazakhstan
B. Turkmenistan
C. Kyrgyzstan
D. Azerbaijan

Ans: B
Diff: M
Page: 809

15. List and analyze Gorbachev's goals for the Soviet Union. Evaluate the practicality of his plans.

Diff: M
Page: 810

16. Outline Osama bin Laden's justification for the September 11, 2001 attack on the United States. What was his message when he appeared on al-Jazeera?

Diff: M
Page: 815

17. In 1979, the Ayatollah Khomeini led a revolution to overthrow the shah of Iran and successfully challenge the power of:
A. France
B. Britain
C. United States
D. Soviet Union

Ans: C
Diff: E
Page: 817

18. In Turkey and Algeria, secular armed forces intervened in elections in the 1990s to prevent political parties from which of the following from coming to power?
A. Christians
B. Jews
C. Hindus
D. Muslims

Ans: D
Diff: E
Page: 817

19. In Nigeria, the proportions of Christians and Muslims is nearly equal, leading to
A. intense Civil War
B. rioting
C. peaceful balance
D. the imposition of an authoritarian dictatorship to control the violence

Ans: B
Diff: M
Page: 818

20. Which of the following was NOT one of the new states created from Yugoslavia after the collapse of the Soviet Union?
A. Bosnia-Herzegovina
B. Serbia
C. Croatia
D. Slovakia

Ans: D
Diff: E
Page: 818

21. Concerning religion and politics, Gandhi claimed that
A. everyone could live under a secular government
B. a Hindu government could peacefully govern all Indians
C. Islam must be eradicated from India
D. Hindus and Muslims must share control of the government

Ans: A
Diff: E
Page: 819

22. The Indian People's Party advocated which of the following when they achieved control?
A. mandating a strict separation of church and state
B. making Hindu identity the basis of national identity
C. reduce the impact of all religions in shaping national identity
D. making Islam the basis of national identity

Ans: B
Diff: E
Page: 819

23. In the 1990s, China experienced a resurgence of
A. Buddhism
B. Islam
C. Confucianism
D. Christianity

Ans: C
Diff: E
Page: 820

24. Forty percent of the world's Jewish population resides:
A. in the United States
B. in Israel
C. in Europe
D. in South America

Ans: A
Diff: E
Page: 821

25. In 2000, somewhat more than a third of a billion Christians live in:
A. Latin America
B. Europe
C. Asia
D. Africa

Ans: D
Diff: E
Page: 821

26. Liberation theology:
A. drew opposition from Pope John Paul II
B. is stronger in Africa than in Latin America
C. is conservative in orientation
D. gains most of its supporters from the middle and upper classes

Ans: A
Diff: M
Page: 823

27. Which of the following is NOT emphasized by Evangelical Christianity?
A. direct, personal experience of God
B. direct revelation
C. the authority of scripture
D. cooperation and material assistance

Ans: C
Diff: M
Pages: 823-824

28. Which of the following approaches was NOT utilized by the Roman Catholic Church in the United States to resolve its sex scandals?
A. training, monitoring, disciplining of clergy
B. willingly turning the problem over to the American legal system
C. public apologies
D. cash payments of restitution

Ans: B
Diff: E
Page: 825

29. T F In the Sudan, civil wars have erupted in response to Sunni attempts to impose Islamic law on the rest of the country.

Ans: T
Diff: M
Page: 817

30. T F Muslims constitute the majority of Bosnia-Herzegovina's population.

Ans: F
Diff: M
Page: 818

31. T F During the struggle for independence in India, the Hindu movement embraced equality for non-Hindus.

Ans: F
Diff: E
Page: 819

32. T F The Chinese government attempted to prohibit the rebirth of Confucianism in the 1990s.

Ans: F
Diff: E
Page: 820

33. T F The Jewish state of Israel has been successful in obtaining peace treaties with Syria and Lebanon.

Ans: F
Diff: M
Page: 821

34. T F Pope John Paul II was the first non-Italian Pope since 1523.

Ans: T
Diff: E
Page: 821

35. T F Evangelical Christianity appeals primarily to the urban poor.

Ans: T
Diff: E
Page: 823

36. T F Christian fundamentalists believe in the literal truth of the bible as a revelation from God.

Ans: T
Diff: E
Page: 824

37. Explain the connection between religious identity and cultural identity. What problems arise in nations with diverse religious beliefs?

Diff: M
Page: 817

38. Describe the impact of immigration on the construction of cultural identity in the United States. What are the positive and negative effects?

Diff: M
Page: 827

39. Compare the findings of Diana Eck and Karen Armstrong concerning religion in the United States. What do you think explains their different perceptions?

Diff: M
Page: 826

40. Critics of "Globalization" claim all of the following, except:
A. it threatens to homogenize the world's cultures
B. it fosters the evolution of enriched economic and cultural patterns
C. it threatens to replace the world's languages with English
D. it is based in the United States so the world's people do not benefit equally

Ans: B
Diff: E
Page: 828

41. According to the text, which of the following is NOT one of the technologies of globalization?
A. radio communication
B. satellite communication
C. the internet
D. the World Wide Web

Ans: A
Diff: E
Page: 828

42. During the 1980s, which major industry had to be bailed out by the government because of bad investments?
A. airlines
B. savings and loan associations
C. railroads
D. telecommunications

Ans: B
Diff: E
Page: 831

43. Which of the following is NOT a goal of the World Social Forum?
A. find alternative economic models
B. find alternative political models
C. underwrite the cost of the forum with funds from major international foundations
D. generate new identities for world development

Ans: C
Diff: E
Page: 833

44. The most widespread, profitable, and largest of all illegal international business is in:
A. drugs
B. weapons
C. sexual slavery
D. technology

Ans: A
Diff: E
Page: 833

45. Most of the women and children sold for sexual slavery come from:
A. South America
B. Southeast Asia
C. Africa
D. Eastern Europe

Ans: B
Diff: E
Page: 834

46. It is illegal to sell weapons to all but which of the following?
A. guerrilla groups
B. NRA members
C. Libya
D. partisans in civil wars

Ans: B
Diff: E
Page: 835

47. The UN convention against Transnational Organize Crime combats all but which of the following?
A. sale of women and children for sexual exploitation
B. smuggling of migrants
C. cultural imperialism by the United States
D. illegal businesses making investments in legal businesses

Ans: C
Diff: M
Page: 836

48. The Human Genome Project is working to
A. clone humans
B. identify the 100,000 genes in human DNA
C. produce blood in the bodies of animals that could be used for human transfusion
D. find a cure for the AIDS virus

Ans: B
Diff: M
Page: 837

49. Which of the following is NOT one of the primary ecological concerns of the United Nations' global agenda?
A. depletion of the ozone layer
B. cigarette smoke
C. global warming
D. Deforestation

Ans: B
Diff: M
Page: 838

50. T F Critics argue that globalization is just one more measure of the superpower status of the United States.

Ans: T
Diff: E
Page: 828

51. T F New technologies decreased the gap between the rich and the poor.

Ans: F
Diff: E
Page: 830

52. T F During the 1980s, the International Monetary Fund came to the rescue of many countries that were experiencing economic depression.

Ans: T
Diff: E
Page: 831

53. T F Illegal immigration into the European Union has dramatically decreased since the fall of the Soviet Union.

Ans: F
Diff: M
Page: 834

54. T F Today, the poor can pay their way out of debt by selling their organs to wealthy transplant recipients.

Ans: T
Diff: E
Page: 834

55. T F Abdul Qadeer Khan, developer of Pakistan's nuclear bomb, admitted to operating a black market in weapons-grade nuclear materials.

Ans: T
Diff: E
Page: 835

56. T F International networks play only a minor role in the global criminal economy.

Ans: F
Diff: E
Page: 836

57. T F Seventy percent of the incidents of AIDS occur in sub-Saharan Africa.

Ans: T
Diff: E
Page: 837

58. T F The destruction of the marine environment through ocean dumping is a major threat to the global ecology.

Ans: T
Diff: E
Page: 838

59. Explain the relationship between technological innovation and the construction of a global identity. In what ways can technological development generate global cooperation, and in what ways can it impede it?

Diff: M
Page: 838

60. Explain the relationship between ecological concerns and the construction of a global identity.

Diff:
Page: 838

61. Compare and contrast the interpretations of globalization offered by Thomas Friedman, Joseph Stiglitz, and Manfred Steger. On what does each base his interpretation? Whose position do you find more convincing? Explain.

Diff: H
Page: 829

1. Which of the following was NOT a goal of the European Economic Community?
A. to ultimately remove tariffs among member countries
B. to foster the free movement of goods, labor and capital
C. to foster the peaceful development of atomic energy
D. to establish a single external tariff

Ans: C
Diff: M
Page: 844

2. The European Union:
A. was formed a year after the end of World War II
B. enriched the economies of its member countries
C. had nine members in 1997
D. was designed primarily to be a military alliance

Ans: B
Diff: M
Page: 845

3. Which of the following is NOT provided by the European Union?
A. finance programs in science and technology
B. support for raising the economic status of its poorer member states
C. basic educational functions
D. standards for health and safety regulations

Ans: C
Diff: M
Page: 845

4. Yugoslavia:
A. was created after World War I.
B. was created after World War II.
C. experienced very little ethnic conflict
D. was a predominantly Muslim country

Ans: A
Diff: E
Page: 846

5. Slobodan Milosevic was all of the following except:
A. president of Serbia
B. responsible for ordering the "ethnic cleansing" of 700,000 Albanians from Kosovo
C. accused of war crimes in the former Yugoslavia
D. re-elected as president of Serbia in 2000

Ans: D
Diff: E
Page: 848

6. T F The European Union brought rapid economic reconstruction and growth to member nations.

Ans: T
Diff: E
Page: 843

7. T F The European Union provides welfare programs for member nations.

Ans: F
Diff: E
Page: 845

8. T F The Serbian government under the leadership of Slobodan Milosevic employed genocide to kill or force out the Muslim and Croat populations, especially from Bosnia.

Ans: T
Diff: E
Page: 847

9. Describe the major accomplishments of the European Union.

Diff: E
Page: 845

10. Describe the actions taken by Milosevic's Serbian government against the Muslims and Croats. How did the world respond to the genocide? How was the UN ultimately able to bring Milosevic before the International War Crimes Tribunal at the Hague?

Diff: M
Pages: 847-848

11. Explain François Mitterrand's perception of the European Union. What connection does he see between the EU and the cultural identity of Europe?

Diff: M
Page: 845

12. South Africa:
A. has a population that is about 45 percent white
B. did not impose the policy of apartheid until the middle of the twentieth century
C. was initially colonized by the British
D. is still the subject of international economic sanctions

Ans: B
Diff: M
Page: 848

13. The United States and other Western countries engaged in all of the following activities against apartheid South Africa, except:
A. giving aid to Marxist guerrillas in front-line states
B. restricting trade
C. ending cultural and sports exchanges
D. withdrawing economic investments

Ans: A
Diff: M
Page: 850

14. After 1990 in South Africa:
A. Nelson Mandela was in jail for four more years
B. a civil war ensued between whites and blacks
C. elections were held using the principle of one person-one vote
D. there was no effort to investigate the abuses of apartheid

Ans: C
Diff: E
Page: 851

15. The two groups committing mutual genocide in Rwanda and Congo were:
A. Hutus and Tutsis
B. Zulus and Sothos
C. Mendes and Mandinkes
D. Shonas and Thongas

Ans: A
Diff: E
Page: 852

16. Laurent Kabila over threw Mobutu Sese Seko in 1997 in this country:
A. Congo (Zaire)
B. Angola
C. Nigeria
D. Uganda

Ans: A
Diff: M
Page: 856

17. T F Most borders in Africa reflect the boundaries between ethnic groups and tribes.

Ans: F
Diff: M
Page: 850

18. T F The Hutu majority controlled Rwanda in 1962.

Ans: T
Diff: E
Page: 855

19. T F The involvement of the United States in the warfare in Congo is limited to behind-the-scenes assistance to whichever side seems most likely to allow American access to Congo's resources.

Ans: T
Diff: E
Page: 856

20. First describe important aspects of the apartheid system, and then move on to a discussion of the evolution of that racist political system into a democratic system.

Diff: M
Pages: 848-852

21. Describe the historic relationship between the Hutus and the Tutsis. What role does European colonization have on the problems in this region? Explain the impact this unrest has had on Congo and Rwanda.

Diff: M
Page: 852-856

22. T F In 1914, Britain dominated most of South Africa.

Ans: T
Diff: E
Page: 849

23. Which of the following is NOT a South African ethnic group?
A. Afrikaans
B. Zulu
C. Bushmen
D. Mende

Ans: D
Diff: M
Page: 850

24. Bantu are most common in this part of Africa:
A. western
B. eastern
C. southern
D. northern

Ans: C
Diff: M
Page: 850

25. Describe the goals of the Truth and Reconciliation Commission in South Africa. Why were many critical of its amnesty policy? What were the commission's positive contributions to South Africa?

Diff: M
Page: 853

26. Latin America:
A. does not usually include the islands of the Caribbean
B. contains about 12 or so countries
C. has a total population of around a half billion
D. has Portuguese as the most common language

Ans: C
Diff: E
Page: 856

27. Which of the following statements about the demographics of Latin America is most true?
A. about half the population lives in cities
B. people are pulled to live in rural areas
C. there is a net movement from rural areas to urban areas
D. immigration to the area has been minimal in the twentieth century

Ans: C
Diff: M
Page: 856

28. The Party of Revolutionary Institutions:
A. was created by Lázaro Cárdenas
B. gave broad representation to the many sectors of Mexican society
C. allowed presidents to serve only two consecutive terms
D. was eventually replaced by a more repressive party

Ans: B
Diff: M
Page: 857

29. This country is NOT part of the North American Free Trade Agreement:
A. Canada
B. Mexico
C. Chile
D. United States

Ans: C
Diff: E
Page: 857

30. Brazilian president Luis Inacio Lula da Silva did all of the following except:
A. distribute land to 500,000 poor families
B. introduce the *bolsa familia* which give $25 each month to poverty stricken families
C. orchestrate a 50 percent increase in the gross national product
D. successfully argue in the World Trade Organization against agricultural subsidies to richer nations

Ans: C
Diff: M
Page: 861

31. T F In the later part of the 1990s, the Party of Revolutionary Institutions gained a majority in Mexico's national legislature.

Ans: F
Diff: M
Page: 857

32. T F Mexican President Vicente Fox was a former Coca-Cola executive.

Ans: T
Diff: E
Page: 859

33. T F Economic inequality is more severe in Brazil than in any other major nation.

Ans: T
Diff: E
Page: 860

34. Write an essay on the Institutional Revolutionary Party (PRI) which discusses and analyzes the following: the sectors of society the party was designed to represent, how the party intended to deal with opposing viewpoints, how it viewed opposition political parties.

Diff: M
Page: 857

35. Describe the major challenges faced by Brazilian president Lula. Evaluate how successful he has been in meeting the needs of the Brazilian citizens.

Diff: M
Page: 861

36. T F Oil is one of the main exports from Venezuela.

Ans: T
Diff: E
Page: 858

37. Under the leadership of Deng Xiaoping, China witnessed all of the following except:
A. improved health standards
B. increased life expectancy
C. dramatic increase in its total gross domestic product
D. an increase in the number of workers employed by the state

Ans: D
Diff: M
Page: 862

38. By 1980, the "small family happiness" program was engaged in all of the following except:
A. distributing contraceptive devices
B. encouraging early marriage
C. monitoring pregnancies
D. mandating abortions

Ans: B
Diff: E
Page: 862

39. Which of the following is NOT one of the "four modernizations" accomplished under Deng's China?
A. agriculture
B. science and technology
C. culture
D. industry

Ans: C
Diff: E
Page: 864

40. The Mandal Commission argued that:
A. caste was the most significant indicator of class
B. castes no longer existed in India
C. castes should no longer be considered in determining public sector employment
D. castes should not be the only criterion in determining eligibility for government positions

Ans: A
Diff: E
Page: 869

41. Upper-caste groups in India are currently more actively involved in which of the following?
A. education
B. religious organizations
C. business careers
D. political offices

Ans: C
Diff: E
Page: 870

42. T F Deng Xiaoping was instrumental in the move toward market economics in China.

Ans: T
Diff: M
Page: 862

43. T F As a result of the "one-family-one-child" policy, female infanticide was sometimes practiced.

Ans: T
Diff: E
Page: 862

44. T F China was censured by the World Health Organization for not immediately reporting the SARS epidemic.

Ans: T
Diff: E
Page: 865

45. T F Information technology is lagging far behind other economic sectors in India today.

Ans: F
Diff: E
Page: 871

46. T F India's new economic identity is based on free markets.

Ans: T
Diff: E
Page: 871

47. What type of social system does India have, and what are its key characteristics? In what ways does the old caste system still shape social, economic, and political relationships?

Diff: H
Pages: 867-870

48. Describe the changes that have been implemented in India's economy since the early 1990s. Evaluate the success of the shift toward a capitalist economy.

Diff: M
Pages: 870-872

49. Contrast economist Amartya Sen's interpretation of the success of Den Xiaoping's economic reforms with that offered by most commentators. What explains his different perspective?

Diff: M
Page: 863

50. Which of the following events was the first to occur?
A. Nelson Mandela was freed
B. Soweto protests
C. Assassination of Yitzhak Rabin
D. Eritrea obtained independence from Ethiopia

Ans: B
Diff: M
Page: 868

51. The Balfour Declaration:
A. pleased both Arabs and Jews
B. called for Jewish immigration to Palestine
C. was the result of a 1947 UN resolution
D. was unambiguous

Ans: B
Diff: M
Page: 873

52. The most important factor spurring the creation of the state of Israel in 1948 was:
A. the virulence of Arab nationalism
B. recent pogroms in Eastern Europe and the Soviet Union
C. the Holocaust
D. the growing importance of the Cold War

Ans: C
Diff: E
Page: 874

53. Which of the following statements about the Arab-Israeli conflict is NOT true?
A. Israel ruled over many Palestinians as a consequence of the 1967 war
B. many Palestinians have become "wandering Jews"
C. Israelis expected Arab states to absorb emigrating Palestinians
D. in the long run, the 1979 peace between Israel and Egypt hurt the peace process

Ans: D
Diff: M
Page: 876

54. Through the Israeli-Palestinian-Arab conflict, which nation historically supported the Arab nations?
A. United States
B. France
C. Soviet Union
D. Britain

Ans: C
Diff: E
Page: 876

55. Movement toward some resolution of the Palestinian-Israeli conflict:
A. led to a formal peace agreement between Israel and Syria in the mid-1990s
B. has yet to give Palestinians any form of political autonomy
C. began when Israel and the Palestinian Liberation Organization recognized each other
D. was opposed by Russia

Ans: C
Diff: M
Page: 877

56. T F Many Arabs felt the creation of Israel was an example European colonialism.

Ans: T
Diff: E
Page: 874

57. T F The 1987 *intifada* employed wide-spread, violent terrorist attacks.

Ans: F
Diff: M
Page: 876

58. T F In response to the second *intifada*, the Israelis began building a physical barrier between Jews and Palestinians.

Ans: T
Diff: E
Page: 878

59. Discuss the Palestinian-Israeli conflict from the Six Day War to the present, with special attention to who controlled or controls what land and what progress has been made in the process of resolving the conflict.

Diff: H
Pages: 875-876

60. The Palestinian-Israeli conflict can be examined through three themes: religious, nationalist, and neocolonial. Write an essay that describes the nature of these themes, why the conflict has been difficult to resolve satisfactorily, and what steps toward peace and accommodation have been taken.

Diff: H
Pages: 873-878

61. Which of the following was the first to achieve independence?
A. Qatar
B. Kuwait
C. Iraq
D. Syria

Ans: C
Diff: M
Page: 872

62. T F Israel more than doubled the size of the area under its control as a result of the Six-Day War.

Ans: T
Diff: M
Page: 875

63. Outline the agreements reached by Israeli Yossi Beilin and Palestinian Abd Rabbo in the Geneva Accords of 2003. Is their proposal practical? Have subsequent events demonstrated that this plan is likely to succeed?

Diff: M
Page: 877